Mastering Pandas in Python: Course Book

Pedro Martins

Published by Pedro Martins, 2024.

MASTERING PANDAS IN PYTHON: COURSE BOOK

First edition. March 17, 2024.

ISBN: 979-8224304905

Written by Pedro Martins.

Dedication

Dedication

To my dear family, whose boundless love and unwavering support have been my beacon of hope and strength. Your sacrifices, encouragement, and belief in my dreams have allowed me to pursue my passion for coding and teaching. This book is a tribute to the endless hours of discussion, the patience in understanding my absence during the countless nights of writing, and the joy we shared in every little success. Your presence in my life is the greatest gift, and this work is just a small token of my appreciation and love for all of you.

And to you, the readers, who embark on this journey to master Pandas with an eager spirit and a willing mind. This book is dedicated to your passion for learning, your commitment to improvement, and your curiosity that drives you to explore the depths of data science. May this course book serve as a reliable companion on your path to mastering Pandas, empowering you to unlock new opportunities and insights within your data.

Together, we share the excitement of discovery and the satisfaction of skill mastery. Thank you for allowing me to be a part of your learning journey. May our paths be enriched by the knowledge we share and the challenges we overcome.

Mastering Pandas in Python: Course Book

Discovery the Panda

Pedro Martins

12.12.2023

Introduction to Pandas

Overview of Pandas

Historical Context

Installation and Getting Started

Creating Data Structures

Data Importing and Handling

Conclusion

Importance of Pandas in Data Analysis

Setting up the Environment for Pandas

Basic Pandas Concepts

2. Data Structures in Pandas

Understanding Series and DataFrames

Creating Series and DataFrames in Pandas

Basic Operations with DataFrames

3. Data Importing and Exporting

Reading Data from Various Sources (CSV, Excel, SQL)

Exporting Data to Different Formats

Handling Missing Data in Pandas

Data Transformation in Pandas

Filtering and Sorting Data in Pandas

Data Type Conversions in Pandas

Basic Statistics with Pandas

Grouping and Aggregating Data in Pandas

Pivot Tables and Cross Tabulations in Pandas

Time Series Analysis in Pandas

FULL EXAMPLE: TIME Series Analysis with Pandas

Generating a Time Series

Time-based Indexing and Slicing

Resampling for Different Frequencies

Visualizing Time Series Data

Conclusion

Reshaping and Pivoting DataFrames in Pandas

Advanced Filtering Techniques in Pandas

Working with Text Data in Pandas

5. Data Visualization with Pandas

Plotting with Pandas

Customizing Plots in Pandas

2. Real-World Projects and Case Studies

Project 1: Analyzing Financial Data

Lab Project: Analyzing Stock Market Data

Objective:

Tools and Libraries:

Project Steps:

Outcome:

Project 2: Data Analysis in Retail

Objective:

Tools and Libraries:

Dataset:

Project Steps:

Outcome:

Lab Project: Retail Data Analysis

Objective:

Tools and Libraries:

Dataset:

Project Steps:

Outcome:

Project 3: Time Series Forecasting

Objective:

Tools and Libraries:

Dataset:

Project Steps:

Outcome:

Lab Project: Time Series Forecasting

Objective:

Tools and Libraries:

Dataset:

Project Steps:

Outcome:

Performance Tuning and Scaling Pandas

1. Using Efficient Data Types:

2. Selecting Columns Wisely:

3. Vectorized Operations:

4. Avoiding Loops:

5. Using Efficient Functions:

6. Incremental Processing:

7. Indexing:

8. Parallel Processing:

9. Memory Management:

10. Query Optimization:

11. Profiling Code:

12. Updating Pandas:

Working with Large Datasets in Pandas

1. Efficient Data Loading:

2. Chunk Processing:

3. Optimize Memory:

4. Filtering Data:

5. Efficient Aggregations and Operations:

6. Using Dask for Parallel Computing:

7. Incremental Loading and Processing:

8. Sampling Data:

9. Utilizing Efficient Storage Formats:

10. Cleaning Up:

Integration with Dask for Parallel Computing in Pandas

How Dask Works with Pandas:

Basic Integration:

Operations with Dask:

Combining Pandas and Dask:

Considerations:

1. Use Vectorized Operations:

2. Avoid Loops When Possible:

3. Use Efficient Data Types:

4. Select Data Efficiently:

5. Use chunksize for Large Files:

6. Avoid Chained Indexing:

7. Use In-Place Operations:

8. Use cat Accessor for Categorical Data:

9. Exploit Pandas Functions:

10. Profile Your Code:

11. Keep Pandas Updated:

12. Consider Parallel Processing for Large Scale Data:

Common Pitfalls in Pandas and How to Avoid Them

1. Inefficient Loops:

2. Chained Assignment:

3. Ignoring Data Types:

4. Incorrect Aggregation or Grouping:

5. Not Handling Missing Data:

6. In-place Modifications:

7. Ignoring Index Alignment:

8. Not Utilizing Datetime Functions:

9. Ignoring Read/Write Options:

10. Overlooking Vectorized String Methods:

11. Not Checking for Duplicate Data:

12. Failing to Profile the Code:

Resources for Further Learning in Pandas

1. Official Pandas Documentation:

2. Books:

3. Online Courses:

4. Interactive Platforms:

5. Tutorials and Blogs:

6. YouTube Channels:

7. Community and Forums:

8. GitHub Repositories:

9. Podcasts:

10. Meetups and Conferences:

11. Jupyter Notebooks:

Appendix: Glossary of Terms in Pandas and Data Analysis

1. DataFrame:

2. Series:

3. Index:

4. NaN:

5. Vectorization:

6. GroupBy:

7. Merge/Join:

8. Concatenation:

9. Dtype:

10. Resampling:

11. Pivot Table:

12. Apply Function:

13. Lambda Function:

14. Cross Tabulation:

15. ARIMA/SARIMA:

16. Correlation:

17. Outlier:

References and Further Reading for Pandas and Data Analysis

Books:

Online Documentation and Tutorials:

Online Courses:

Video Tutorials:

Forums and Community:

Research Papers and Articles:

Index

Introduction to Pandas

Overview of Pandas

Pandas is an essential library in Python's data science stack, revered for its robust capabilities in data manipulation and analysis. As a cornerstone tool for Python programmers, especially in the realms of data science, finance, and analytics, Pandas has revolutionized the way data is handled and analyzed in Python.

Key Features:

- **Data Structures:** At the heart of Pandas are two primary data structures: Series (one-dimensional arrays) and DataFrames (two-dimensional tables). These structures are capable of handling a wide array of data types and are optimized for performance, even with large datasets.

- **Data Manipulation:** Pandas simplifies tasks such as data importing, cleaning, and filtering. It offers intuitive ways to index, slice, reshape, and pivot data, making data manipulation tasks less cumbersome.

- **Data Analysis:** Beyond basic data manipulation, Pandas provides powerful tools for in-depth analysis. This includes functions for aggregation, summary statistics, and time-series analysis, enabling sophisticated data operations with minimal code.

- **Integration with Other Libraries:** Pandas seamlessly integrates with various data sources and formats, including SQL databases, Excel spreadsheets, and CSV files. It also works well with other libraries in the Python data ecosystem, such as NumPy for numerical computing and Matplotlib for data visualization.

Historical Context

DEVELOPED BY WES MCKINNEY in 2008, Pandas was conceived out of the need for a more flexible and efficient tool for data analysis in Python. McKinney, working in finance at the time, required a tool that could handle the rigors of financial data analysis. The development of Pandas filled this gap, and it quickly became a fundamental tool in data analysis across various fields.

Installation and Getting Started

INSTALLING PANDAS IS straightforward, usually involving a simple pip command:

pip install pandas

Once installed, you can import Pandas, typically using the alias pd:

import pandas as pd

Creating Data Structures

CREATING A BASIC DATAFRAME:

data = {

'Name': ['Alice', 'Bob', 'Charles'],

'Age': [25, 30, 35],

'City': ['New York', 'Paris', 'London']

}

df = pd.DataFrame(data)

print(df)

The DataFrame created from our provided data looks like this:

```
Name Age City

0 Alice 25 New York

1 Bob 30 Paris

2 Charles 35 London
```

It includes columns for "Name", "Age", and "City" with the respective values we've provided. You can test your code directly in an online Python editor by using https://onecompiler.com/python/ . Simply copy this code snippet into the editor, and you will see the previously mentioned result in the OneCompiler editor.

Python Online Compiler

Write, Run & Share Python code online using OneCompiler's Python online compiler for free. It's one of the robust, feature-rich online compilers for python language, supporting both the versions which are Python 3 and Python 2.7. Getting started with the OneCompiler's Python

Data Importing and Handling

PANDAS SHINES IN ITS ability to read and write data in various formats. For example, reading a CSV file is as simple as:

df = pd.read_csv('path/to/your/file.csv')

Similarly, exporting a DataFrame to an Excel file is straightforward:

df.to_excel('path/to/your/output.xlsx')

Conclusion

PANDAS' SIGNIFICANCE in the Python ecosystem cannot be overstated. It provides an efficient, intuitive, and versatile framework for data manipulation and analysis, making it an indispensable tool for anyone delving into data science or analytics with Python.

Importance of Pandas in Data Analysis

PANDAS, A LINCHPIN in the Python data analysis toolkit, has gained immense popularity and importance due to its powerful features and ease of use. Its significance in the realm of data analysis can be understood through several key aspects:

1. **Simplifying Data Manipulation:** In data analysis, a significant amount of time is devoted to preparing data – cleaning, transforming, and reshaping it. Pandas excels in these areas, offering a wide range of functionalities that simplify these tasks, making data manipulation more efficient and less error-prone.
2. **Handling Large Datasets:** Pandas is designed to work efficiently with large datasets. It can handle large volumes of data with ease, performing operations like sorting, filtering, and aggregating swiftly. This capability is crucial in the era of big data, where analysts often work with extensive datasets.
3. **Integrated Data Analysis Tools:** Beyond basic data manipulation, Pandas provides integrated functions for complex data analysis tasks. This includes capabilities for grouping data, generating pivot tables, performing time-series analysis, and computing summary statistics. These integrated tools allow analysts to draw insights from data without needing to switch contexts or tools.
4. **Seamless Data Import and Export:** Pandas supports a wide range of file formats for data import and export, including CSV, Excel, JSON, HTML, and SQL databases. This versatility makes it an indispensable tool for analysts who often work with data in various formats from different sources.
5. **Time Series Analysis:** Pandas has robust features for working with time-series data — essential in many fields like finance, economics, and meteorology. It simplifies tasks like date range generation, frequency conversion, moving window statistics, and date shifting.
6. **Interoperability with Other Python Libraries:** Pandas integrates seamlessly with other libraries in the Python data ecosystem, such as NumPy for numerical computations, Matplotlib and Seaborn for data visualization, and Scikit-learn for machine learning. This interoperability makes it a central component in a data analyst's toolkit.
7. **Community and Ecosystem:** As an open-source tool, Pandas has a strong community support and a wealth of resources available. The active development and extensive documentation make it accessible for beginners, while its depth of functionality caters to the needs of experienced analysts.
8. **Facilitating Data-driven Decision Making:** By enabling efficient data analysis, Pandas plays a crucial role in helping organizations make informed, data-driven decisions. It allows analysts to quickly transform raw data into actionable insights, a critical capability in today's data-centric world.

Setting up the Environment for Pandas

SETTING UP A PROPER environment for using Pandas in Python is a crucial initial step in data analysis. This process involves installing Python, setting up a suitable environment, and installing Pandas along with other essential libraries. Here's a guide to get you started:

1. Install Python:

○ Ensure Python is installed on your system. Python 3.x is recommended as it's the latest and has more features and support.

○ You can download Python from the official website: python.org[1].

2. Choose an Integrated Development Environment (IDE):

○ Select an IDE or a text editor for writing your Python code. Popular choices include Jupyter Notebook, PyCharm, Visual Studio Code, or even a simple text editor like Sublime Text.

○ Jupyter Notebook is particularly popular for data analysis as it allows you to write code, view outputs, and add annotations in one place.

3. Set Up a Virtual Environment (Optional but Recommended):

○ A virtual environment is a self-contained directory that contains a Python installation for a particular version of Python, plus a number of additional packages.

○ This keeps your project's dependencies separate from other projects, avoiding version conflicts.

○ Use tools like venv (built-in), virtualenv, or conda (if using Anaconda) to create virtual environments.

To create a virtual environment with venv:

```
python -m venv my_project_env
```

○ Activate the environment:

- On Windows: my_project_env\Scripts\activate

- On macOS and Linux: source my_project_env/bin/activate

4. Install Pandas and Other Essential Libraries:

Once your environment is set up, install Pandas using pip:

```
pip install pandas
```

○ Consider installing other useful libraries for data analysis, such as NumPy for numerical operations, Matplotlib and Seaborn for data visualization, and SciPy for scientific computing.

5. Running a Test Script:

Test your setup by running a simple Pandas script. For example, in your Python IDE or text editor, try the following:

```
import pandas as pd
df = pd.DataFrame({'A': [1, 2, 3], 'B': [4, 5, 6]})
print(df)
```

This script creates a simple DataFrame and prints it.

6. Explore Additional Resources:

---

1. https://www.python.org/downloads/

○ Explore tutorials and documentation to get comfortable with Pandas. The official Pandas documentation[2] is an excellent place to start.

By following these steps, you'll have a robust environment set up for working with Pandas and performing data analysis in Python. This setup will serve as a strong foundation for exploring the vast capabilities of Pandas and other Python data analysis tools. In summary, Pandas is not just a tool but a foundational framework in Python for data analysis. Its comprehensive capabilities for data manipulation, analysis, and its integration within the wider data science ecosystem make it an indispensable asset for data analysts and scientists.

Basic Pandas Concepts

PANDAS, A CORNERSTONE of data analysis in Python, provides powerful and flexible tools to work with structured data. Here are some fundamental concepts and functionalities in Pandas that are essential for any data analyst to understand:

1. **Pandas Data Structures:**

Series: A one-dimensional labeled array capable of holding any data type (integers, strings, floating point numbers, Python objects, etc.). It's similar to a column in a spreadsheet.

import pandas as pd

series = pd.Series([1, 3, 5, 7, 9])

The Pandas Series you've created is as follows:

```

0 1

1 3

2 5

3 7

4 9

dtype: int64

```

This Series consists of integers 1, 3, 5, 7, and 9, each indexed from 0 to 4.

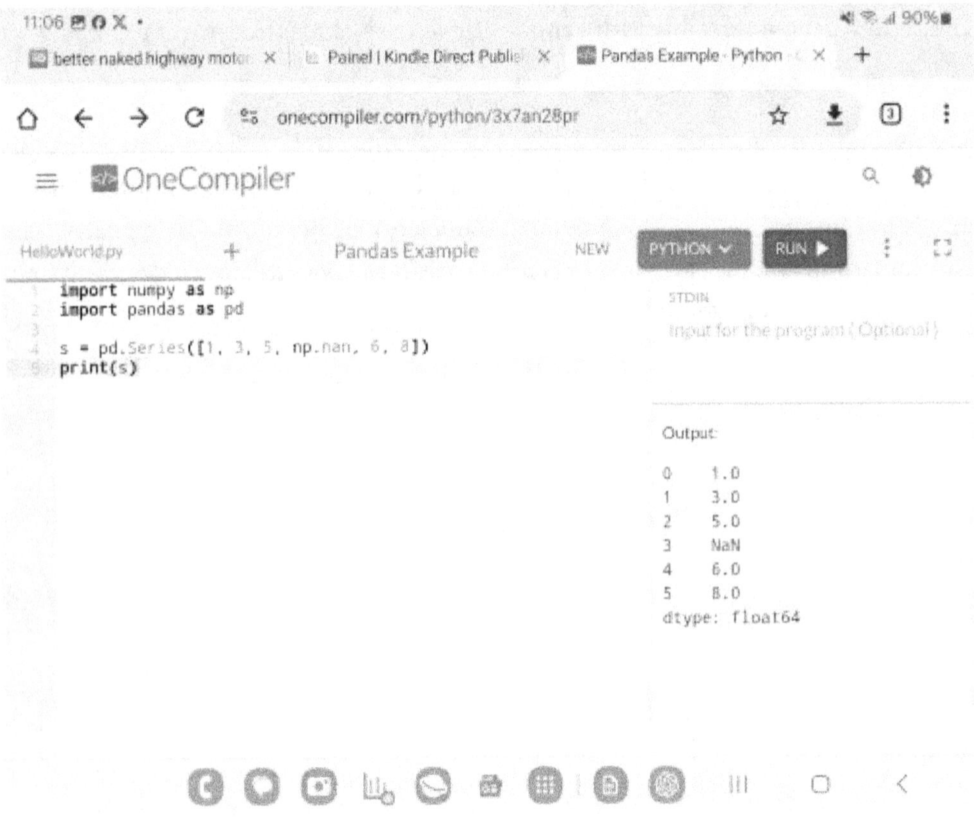

DataFrame: A two-dimensional, size-mutable, and potentially heterogeneous tabular data structure with labeled axes (rows and columns). It resembles a spreadsheet or SQL table.

data = {'Name': ['Alice', 'Bob', 'Chris'], 'Age': [25, 30, 35]}

df = pd.DataFrame(data)

The DataFrame you've created from the provided data looks like this:

```

Name Age

0 Alice 25

1 Bob 30

2 Chris 35

```

It includes a "Name" column with the values Alice, Bob, and Chris, and an "Age" column with the values 25, 30, and 35, respectively. In the OneCompiler the result is:

2. Indexing and Selection:

○ Accessing data in Pandas is straightforward. You can select, index, and assign data in a DataFrame using methods like .loc[], .iloc[], and direct slicing.

○ .loc[] is label-based indexing, which means that you have to specify the name of the rows and columns that you need to filter out.

○ .iloc[] is integer index-based. You use integer indexes to select data.

3. Data Importing and Exporting:

○ Pandas supports various file formats for importing and exporting data, including CSV, Excel, and JSON.

○ For example, pd.read_csv('filename.csv') to read a CSV file into a DataFrame, and df.to_csv('filename.csv') to write a DataFrame to a CSV file.

4. Data Cleaning:

○ Data cleaning functions include handling missing data, dropping or filling NA values, and type conversion.

○ Methods like df.dropna(), df.fillna(), and df.astype() are commonly used for these tasks.

5. Data Exploration:

○ Pandas provides functions for a quick look at your data, like df.head(), df.tail(), df.describe(), which are useful for getting a sense of the data structure and statistics.

6. **Data Manipulation:**

○ Operations like merging, joining, concatenation, and changing the shape of data are integral parts of data analysis.

○ Functions such as pd.concat(), df.merge(), and df.pivot_table() are used for such manipulations.

7. **Grouping and Aggregation:**

○ Grouping data based on some criteria and then computing aggregate statistics is a common task in data analysis.

○ Using df.groupby() followed by an aggregation method like .sum(), .mean(), etc., is a powerful way to analyze subsets of data.

8. **Time Series Analysis:**

○ Pandas has specialized time series functionalities, such as date range generation, frequency conversion, window functions, and lagging and differencing.

9. **Visualization:**

○ Although Pandas is not primarily a visualization library, it provides basic capabilities to create charts from DataFrames, integrating closely with libraries like Matplotlib.

Understanding these core concepts forms the foundation of data manipulation and analysis with Pandas in Python. With these tools, you can tackle a wide array of data processing tasks, paving the way for more advanced data analysis and machine learning applications.

2. Data Structures in Pandas

Understanding Series and DataFrames

Pandas provides two key data structures: Series and DataFrame, which are built on top of NumPy and designed for efficient data manipulation.

Series:

1. **Definition:** A Series is a one-dimensional array-like object containing a sequence of values (similar to a NumPy array) and an associated array of data labels, called its index. Essentially, a Series is a single column of data.

Creation: A Series can be created from a list, an array, or a dictionary. For example:

import pandas as pd

From a list

s1 = pd.Series([1, 3, 5, 7, 9])

From a dictionary

s2 = pd.Series({'a': 1, 'b': 2, 'c': 3})

Here are the outputs for the two Series you've created:

Series from a list (`s1`):

```
0 1
1 3
2 5
3 7
4 9
dtype: int64
```

Series from a dictionary (`s2`):

```
```

```
a 1

b 2

c 3

dtype: int64
```

```

The first Series (`s1`) is indexed automatically from 0 to 4 with the values 1, 3, 5, 7, and 9. The second Series (`s2`) uses the dictionary keys 'a', 'b', and 'c' as its index with the corresponding values 1, 2, and 3. In the IDE editor OneCompiler the result will be:

Python Online Compiler

2. **Features:**

○ **Indexing:** Each item in a Series has a unique index, which can be numeric or label-based.

○ **Heterogeneous Data:** A Series can hold data of any type supported by NumPy.

○ **Vectorized Operations:** You can apply functions and perform operations on a Series in a vectorized way.

3. **Usage:** Series are useful for time-series data, individual columns in datasets, and any other form of sequential data.

**DataFrames:**

1. **Definition:** A DataFrame is a two-dimensional, size-mutable, and potentially heterogeneous tabular data structure with labeled axes (rows and columns). It can be thought of as a spreadsheet or SQL table.
```

Creation: DataFrames can be created from dictionaries of Series, lists, arrays, or even other DataFrames. For example:

From a dictionary of lists/arrays

df = pd.DataFrame({'A': [1, 2, 3], 'B': [4, 5, 6]})

2. **Features:**

○ **Versatile Indexing:** Like Series, DataFrames have row and column labels for indexing.

○ **Handling of Missing Data:** Pandas automatically aligns data and handles missing values.

○ **Flexible Reshaping:** You can pivot, stack, or rearrange data easily.

○ **Rich Functionality:** DataFrames come with numerous built-in methods for aggregation, filtering, and visualization.

3. **Usage:** DataFrames are the workhorse of data analysis tasks in Pandas. They're used for data cleaning, preparation, analysis, and visualization.

Both Series and DataFrames are integral to data analysis in Pandas. Understanding these structures is key to manipulating, analyzing, and visualizing data effectively.

Creating Series and DataFrames in Pandas

UNDERSTANDING HOW TO create Series and DataFrames is fundamental in using Pandas for data analysis. These structures form the backbone of most operations you'll perform with Pandas.

Creating a Series:

1. **From a List:**

○ A simple way to create a Series is from a Python list.

import pandas as pd

data = [1, 3, 5, 7, 9]

series = pd.Series(data)

2. **From a Dictionary:**

○ When creating a Series from a dictionary, the keys become the Series index.

data = {'a': 1, 'b': 2, 'c': 3}

series = pd.Series(data)

3. **With Custom Index:**

○ You can specify an index separately from the data.

data = [1, 3, 5, 7, 9]

index = ['A', 'B', 'C', 'D', 'E']

series = pd.Series(data, index=index)

The Pandas Series you've created with specified data and custom index looks like this:

```
\ \ \

A 1

B 3

C 5

D 7

E 9

dtype: int64

\ \ \
```

This Series has the values 1, 3, 5, 7, and 9, each associated with a custom index of 'A', 'B', 'C', 'D', and 'E', respectively. The result in the Editor:

Creating a DataFrame:

1. From a Dictionary of Lists:

○ Each key-value pair in the dictionary becomes a column in the DataFrame.

data = {

'Name': ['Alice', 'Bob', 'Charlie'],

'Age': [25, 30, 35],

'City': ['New York', 'Paris', 'London']

}

df = pd.DataFrame(data)

The DataFrame created from your provided data looks like this:

```

Name Age City

0 Alice 25 New York

1 Bob 30 Paris

2 Charlie 35 London

```

It includes columns for "Name", "Age", and "City" with the respective values you've provided for each individual. Lets see the result in the editor:

2. **From a List of Dictionaries:**

Each dictionary in the list becomes a row in the DataFrame.

data = [

{'Name': 'Alice', 'Age': 25, 'City': 'New York'},

{'Name': 'Bob', 'Age': 30, 'City': 'Paris'},

{'Name': 'Charlie', 'Age': 35, 'City': 'London'}

]

df = pd.DataFrame(data)

The DataFrame created from your list of dictionaries looks like this:

```

Name Age City

0 Alice 25 New York

1 Bob 30 Paris

2 Charlie 35 London

```

Each dictionary in the list corresponds to a row in the DataFrame, with "Name", "Age", and "City" as the columns and their respective values from the dictionaries. In the editor:

3. From a List of Lists with Columns:

○ You can provide the data as a list of lists (or tuples) and separately specify column names.

data = [

['Alice', 25, 'New York'],

```
['Bob', 30, 'Paris'],

['Charlie', 35, 'London']

]

columns = ['Name', 'Age', 'City']

df = pd.DataFrame(data, columns=columns)
```

The DataFrame you've created with the provided data and column names looks like this:

```
Name Age City

0 Alice 25 New York

1 Bob 30 Paris

2 Charlie 35 London
```

It includes three columns, "Name", "Age", and "City", with each row corresponding to the values provided in your list of lists. In the editor the full example will be:

4. From a Series:

○ A DataFrame can also be created from one or more Series.

```
series1 = pd.Series(['Alice', 'Bob', 'Charlie'])

series2 = pd.Series([25, 30, 35])
```

df = pd.DataFrame({'Name': series1, 'Age': series2})

The DataFrame created from the two Series looks like this:

```

Name Age

0 Alice 25

1 Bob 30

2 Charlie 35

```

The first Series provided the values for the "Name" column, and the second Series provided the values for the "Age" column. Each row corresponds to the respective positions of the values in the Series. Full example in the editor will see:

In conclusion, these methods provide flexibility in creating Series and DataFrames, allowing you to handle data in various formats effectively. As you become more familiar with Pandas, you'll find that these structures are highly adaptable to the needs of your data analysis tasks.

Basic Operations with DataFrames

ONCE YOU HAVE CREATED DataFrames in Pandas, the next step is to perform basic operations. These operations include viewing the data, selecting specific data, adding or deleting columns and rows, and modifying the data. Understanding these operations is essential for data manipulation and analysis.

    1. **Viewing Data:**

○ **Head and Tail:** Use df.head(n) to view the first n rows and df.tail(n) for the last n rows. If n is omitted, it defaults to 5.

df.head() # First 5 rows

df.tail(3) # Last 3 rows

○ **Display the Index and Columns:** Use df.index and df.columns to view the index and columns of the DataFrame.

df.index # Display the index

df.columns # Display the column names

2. **Selection:**

○ **Selecting Columns:** Columns can be selected using column names.

df['ColumnName'] # Returns a Series

df[['Col1', 'Col2']] # Returns a DataFrame with specified columns

○ **Row Selection Using iloc and loc:**

▪ iloc is used for selection by integer index.

▪ loc is used for selection by label.

df.iloc[0] # First row of DataFrame

df.loc['index1'] # Row with label 'index1'

3. **Adding and Deleting Columns:**

○ **Adding New Columns:** You can add new columns by assigning data to them.

df['NewColumn'] = [value1, value2, value3]

○ **Deleting Columns:** Use del or df.drop().

del df['ColumnToRemove']

df.drop('ColumnToRemove', axis=1, inplace=True)

4. **Modifying Data:**

○ You can modify data in a DataFrame by assigning new values to specific cells.

df.loc['RowIndex', 'ColumnName'] = newValue

5. **Sorting and Filtering:**

○ **Sorting:** Use df.sort_values(by='ColumnName') to sort the DataFrame by a specific column.

df.sort_values(by='Age', ascending=False)

○ **Filtering:** You can use conditions to filter rows.

df[df['Age'] > 30] # Rows where age is greater than 30

6. **Aggregations and Statistics:**

○ Use methods like sum(), mean(), median(), min(), max(), etc., for aggregations.

df['Age'].mean() # Average of the 'Age' column

df.describe() # Summary statistics for numerical columns

7. **Handling Missing Values:**

○ Use df.isna(), df.dropna(), and df.fillna() for dealing with missing data.

df.isna() # Checks for missing values

df.dropna() # Drops rows with missing values

df.fillna(value=0) # Fills missing values with 0

Understanding these basic operations equips you with the tools to start exploring and analyzing your data using Pandas. As you delve deeper into data analysis, you'll find these operations indispensable in your daily tasks.

3. Data Importing and Exporting

Reading Data from Various Sources (CSV, Excel, SQL)

Pandas provides a wide range of functions to read data from various sources like CSV files, Excel spreadsheets, and SQL databases. These functionalities make it extremely versatile and efficient in handling diverse data formats.

1. Reading from CSV Files:

- CSV (Comma Separated Values) files are one of the most common data formats in data analysis.

- Use pd.read_csv() to read a CSV file into a DataFrame.

import pandas as pd

df = pd.read_csv('path/to/your/file.csv')

- You can specify various parameters like delimiter, column names, data types, and more.

2. Reading from Excel Files:

- Excel files are also widely used, especially in business contexts.

- Use pd.read_excel() to read data from Excel files.

df = pd.read_excel('path/to/your/file.xlsx', sheet_name='Sheet1')

- This function allows you to specify the sheet name or number, data format, and other Excel-specific options.

3. Reading from SQL Databases:

- For data stored in SQL databases, Pandas can connect to the database and query data directly.

- Use pd.read_sql() or pd.read_sql_query() to read data from a SQL database.

import sqlalchemy

engine = sqlalchemy.create_engine('database_url')

df = pd.read_sql('SELECT * FROM your_table', engine)

- You'll need to create a connection engine using SQLAlchemy or a similar library, depending on your database.

Exporting Data:

Pandas also provides functions to export DataFrames to various formats, making it easy to share data or use it in different applications.

1. **To CSV:**

   ○ Export a DataFrame to a CSV file using df.to_csv().

df.to_csv('path/to/your/output.csv')

2. **To Excel:**

   ○ Export to an Excel file using df.to_excel().

df.to_excel('path/to/your/output.xlsx')

3. **To SQL Database:**

   ○ Write data to a SQL database using df.to_sql().

df.to_sql('your_table', engine)

The ability to import and export data easily in various formats is one of the key strengths of Pandas, making it an invaluable tool for data analysts and scientists who work with a variety of data sources.

Exporting Data to Different Formats

PANDAS PROVIDES ROBUST functionalities for exporting data to various formats, enabling seamless integration with different systems and tools. Here's how you can export data from Pandas DataFrames to some commonly used formats:

1. Exporting to CSV:

   ● CSV (Comma-Separated Values) is a widely used format for storing tabular data.

   ● Use df.to_csv() to export a DataFrame to a CSV file.

df.to_csv('output.csv', index=False)

   ● The index=False parameter is optional and is used to prevent writing row indices into the CSV file.

2. Exporting to Excel:

   ● Excel files are commonly used in business environments.

   ● Use df.to_excel() to export a DataFrame to an Excel file.

df.to_excel('output.xlsx', sheet_name='Sheet1')

   ● You can specify the sheet name and other Excel-specific options.

3. Exporting to JSON:

- JSON (JavaScript Object Notation) is a lightweight data-interchange format, often used in web applications.

- Use df.to_json() to export a DataFrame to a JSON file.

df.to_json('output.json')

- Pandas provides options to format the JSON output.

4. Exporting to HTML:

- Exporting to HTML can be useful for creating web-readable tables.

- Use df.to_html() to export a DataFrame to an HTML file.

df.to_html('output.html')

- This is particularly useful for presenting data in a more readable format on web pages.

5. Exporting to SQL Database:

- For integration with relational databases, Pandas can export DataFrames directly to SQL tables.

- Use df.to_sql() to export data to a SQL database.

import sqlalchemy

engine = sqlalchemy.create_engine('database_url')

df.to_sql('table_name', con=engine)

- You need to set up a connection to the database first, which can be done using SQLAlchemy or similar libraries.

6. Exporting to Other Formats:

- Pandas also supports other formats like Parquet, HDF5, and more, catering to specific needs like efficient storage and retrieval of large datasets.

Considerations When Exporting:

- **Data Types:** Ensure that the data types are compatible with the format you're exporting to.

- **Large Data:** For very large datasets, consider formats like Parquet, which are optimized for size and performance.

- **Privacy and Security:** When exporting data, especially in formats like Excel or CSV, be mindful of sensitive information and apply necessary data anonymization or encryption.

Exporting data to different formats is a crucial aspect of data analysis, as it allows for the sharing of insights and integration of data science workflows with other business processes. Pandas, with its versatile export options, makes this task efficient and flexible.

1. Data Cleaning and Preparation

Handling Missing Data in Pandas

ONE OF THE MOST COMMON challenges in data analysis is dealing with missing data. Pandas offers a variety of tools to handle missing data effectively, which is crucial for ensuring the accuracy and integrity of your analysis.

1. Identifying Missing Data:

- Use df.isna() or df.isnull() to check for missing values, which returns a DataFrame of boolean values indicating the presence of missing data.

missing_values = df.isna()

- To count the number of missing values in each column, combine isna() with sum().

missing_count = df.isna().sum()

2. Removing Missing Data:

- Use df.dropna() to remove rows or columns containing missing values.

df_cleaned = df.dropna() # Drops rows with any missing value

df_cleaned = df.dropna(axis=1) # Drops columns with any missing value

- This method is straightforward but can result in significant data loss, especially if your dataset has a lot of missing values.

3. Filling Missing Data:

- Use df.fillna() to fill missing values with a specified value or method.

df_filled = df.fillna(0) # Fill missing values with 0

df_filled = df.fillna(method='ffill') # Forward fill

df_filled = df.fillna(method='bfill') # Backward fill

- Forward fill (ffill) fills missing values with the previous valid value, while backward fill (bfill) uses the next valid value.

4. Interpolation:

- Interpolation is a technique to fill missing values according to different methods.

df_interpolated = df.interpolate(method='linear')

- This is particularly useful for time-series data where you can interpolate missing values based on surrounding data points.

5. Replacing Values:

- Use df.replace() to replace missing values or any other value with a specified value.

df_replaced = df.replace(to_replace=np.nan, value=0)

6. Handling Missing Data in Specific Columns:

- You might want to fill or drop missing values only in specific columns. This can be done by applying these methods to particular DataFrame columns.

df['column'] = df['column'].fillna(value)

Best Practices:

- **Understand the Context:** Before handling missing data, understand why it is missing and how it impacts your analysis.

- **Avoid Excessive Data Loss:** Be cautious with methods that remove data. Sometimes, it's better to fill missing values rather than losing data rows.

- **Appropriate Filling:** Choose a filling method that makes sense for your data. For example, using the mean or median to fill missing numerical data, or a constant value like 'Unknown' for categorical data.

- **Consistency:** Ensure consistent handling of missing data across your dataset to avoid biases in your analysis.

Handling missing data effectively is crucial for maintaining the quality of your data analysis. Pandas provides versatile tools for this, allowing you to make informed decisions based on the nature of your data and the requirements of your analysis.

Data Transformation in Pandas

DATA TRANSFORMATION involves modifying data structures and values to make them more suitable for analysis. Pandas offers a wide range of functionalities for efficient and effective data transformation.

1. Column Operations:

Creating New Columns: New columns can be created based on existing data.

df['NewColumn'] = df['Column1'] + df['Column2']

Applying Functions: Use .apply() to apply a function to each element in a column.

```python
df['ProcessedColumn'] = df['OriginalColumn'].apply(lambda x: x * 2)
```

2. Row Operations:

Adding Rows: Concatenate rows from another DataFrame or append individual rows.

```python
df = pd.concat([df, new_df])
```

```python
df = df.append(new_row, ignore_index=True)
```

Dropping Rows: Remove rows based on conditions.

```python
df = df.drop(df[df['Column'] < threshold].index)
```

3. Data Type Conversion:

Change the data type of a column with .astype().

```python
df['Column'] = df['Column'].astype('float')
```

4. Handling Categorical Data:

Convert categorical data into dummy/indicator variables.

```python
df = pd.get_dummies(df, columns=['CategoryColumn'])
```

5. Normalization and Standardization:

Standardize or normalize data, especially useful in machine learning.

```python
df['Normalized'] = (df['Column'] - df['Column'].mean()) / df['Column'].std()
```

6. String Operations:

Extensive support for vectorized string operations without needing for loops.

```python
df['Processed'] = df['TextColumn'].str.lower()
```

7. Handling Date and Time:

Convert strings to datetime objects and extract date or time components.

```python
df['Date'] = pd.to_datetime(df['DateString'])
```

```python
df['Year'] = df['Date'].dt.year
```

8. Grouping and Aggregation:

Group data and apply aggregate functions like sum, mean, etc.

```python
grouped = df.groupby('GroupColumn').sum()
```

9. Reshaping Data:

Use pivot tables, stacking, and unstacking to reshape data.

df_pivot = df.pivot_table(index='IndexColumn', columns='Columns', values='Value')

10. Merging and Joining:

Combine data from different DataFrames based on a common key.

merged_df = pd.merge(df1, df2, on='KeyColumn')

11. Filtering Data:

Use conditions to filter out rows.

filtered_df = df[df['Column'] > threshold]

12. Sorting Data:

Sort data by one or more columns.

df = df.sort_values(by=['Column1', 'Column2'], ascending=[True, False])

Data transformation is a critical step in preparing your dataset for analysis. Pandas provides a robust and versatile toolkit for these tasks, allowing you to manipulate data in ways that best suit your analytical needs.

Filtering and Sorting Data in Pandas

FILTERING AND SORTING are key data manipulation tasks in Pandas, enabling you to organize and focus on specific segments of your data. These operations enhance the ability to perform targeted analyses and gain insights.

Filtering Data:

    1. Using Conditions:

      ○ You can filter data using conditions based on column values.

filtered_df = df[df['Age'] > 30] # Rows where age is greater than 30

    2. Multiple Conditions:

      ○ Combine multiple conditions using & (and) or | (or).

filtered_df = df[(df['Age'] > 30) & (df['City'] == 'New York')]

    3. Using query:

      ○ The query method offers a more readable way to filter data.

filtered_df = df.query('Age > 30 & City == "New York"')

4. **Filtering with isin:**

○ Useful for filtering data based on a list of values.

filtered_df = df[df['City'].isin(['New York', 'London'])]

Sorting Data:

1. **Sorting by a Column:**

○ Use sort_values to sort data by one or more columns.

sorted_df = df.sort_values(by='Age')

2. **Sorting in Descending Order:**

○ Set ascending to False to sort in descending order.

sorted_df = df.sort_values(by='Age', ascending=False)

3. **Sorting by Multiple Columns:**

○ Specify a list of columns to sort by multiple columns.

sorted_df = df.sort_values(by=['City', 'Age'])

4. **Sorting by Index:**

○ Use sort_index to sort by the DataFrame index.

sorted_df = df.sort_index()

Combining Filtering and Sorting:

● You can combine both filtering and sorting to refine your data analysis further.

refined_df = df[df['Age'] > 30].sort_values(by='Age')

Filtering and sorting are fundamental to preparing your data for analysis, allowing you to quickly isolate and order your data as needed for your specific analytical tasks. These operations in Pandas are not only powerful but also intuitive, making data manipulation a more streamlined process.

Data Type Conversions in Pandas

IN PANDAS, CONVERTING the data types of columns is a common operation, especially when you're preparing data for analysis or machine learning models. Proper data types ensure that operations on the DataFrame are appropriate and efficient.

1. Converting Data Types with astype:

- The astype() method is used to explicitly convert data types from one to another.

df['column_name'] = df['column_name'].astype('desired_type')

- For example, converting a column to a string type:

df['column_name'] = df['column_name'].astype(str)

- Or to a float:

df['column_name'] = df['column_name'].astype(float)

2. Converting to Numeric Types:

- Use pd.to_numeric() for converting columns to numeric types, which is useful when dealing with mixed types in a column.

df['column_name'] = pd.to_numeric(df['column_name'], errors='coerce')

- The errors='coerce' parameter will replace non-numeric values with NaN.

3. Converting Dates and Times:

- If you're working with time-series data, converting strings to datetime objects is common.

df['date_column'] = pd.to_datetime(df['date_column'])

- This conversion allows you to leverage Pandas' powerful time-series functionality.

4. Handling Categorical Data:

- Convert a column to a categorical type using astype('category'). This can save memory and often speeds up computations.

df['category_column'] = df['category_column'].astype('category')

5. Converting Booleans:

- Columns can be converted to boolean types, where appropriate.

df['bool_column'] = df['bool_column'].astype(bool)

6. Handling Missing or Incorrect Data:

- Sometimes, data type conversions may fail due to missing or incorrect data. Ensure that the data is clean and formatted correctly before converting types.

7. Checking Data Types:

- Use df.dtypes to check the data types of all columns in a DataFrame.

```
print(df.dtypes)
```

Data type conversions are crucial in the data preparation process. They ensure that each column in your DataFrame is of the correct type for your specific analysis or modeling task, leading to more reliable and efficient operations.

1. Data Analysis and Exploration

Basic Statistics with Pandas

PANDAS PROVIDES A WIDE range of functions to calculate basic statistical measures, which are essential for understanding the characteristics and distribution of your data. Here's how you can use Pandas to perform basic statistical analysis:

1. Descriptive Statistics:

describe(): This method provides a summary of the central tendency, dispersion, and shape of a dataset's distribution.

```
df.describe()
```

    ○ By default, it includes only numeric columns. You can include other data types with the include parameter.

2. Measures of Central Tendency:

Mean: Calculate the mean of a column.

```
df['column'].mean()
```

Median: Compute the median.

```
df['column'].median()
```

3. Measures of Dispersion:

Standard Deviation: Determine the standard deviation.

```
df['column'].std()
```

Variance: Compute the variance.

```
df['column'].var()
```

Range: Find the range (difference between max and min).

```
range = df['column'].max() - df['column'].min()
```

Quantiles: Calculate quantiles.

```
df['column'].quantile([0.25, 0.5, 0.75])
```

4. Measures of Shape:

Skewness: Assess the asymmetry of the data distribution.

df['column'].skew()

Kurtosis: Measure the "tailedness" of the data distribution.

df['column'].kurtosis()

5. Counting Values:

Value Counts: Useful for categorical data to count the number of occurrences of each unique value.

df['categorical_column'].value_counts()

6. Correlation and Covariance:

Correlation: Assess the relationship between variables.

df.corr()

Covariance: Measure how changes in one variable are associated with changes in another.

df.cov()

7. Aggregate Functions:

Use agg() to apply multiple statistical functions to columns.

df.agg({

'column1': ['mean', 'min', 'max'],

'column2': ['median', 'std']

})

8. Grouped Statistics:

Group data and calculate statistics for each group with groupby().

df.groupby('group_column').mean()

Understanding these basic statistical methods is crucial for data analysis, as they provide insights into the nature and quality of your data. They are the first step in any data analysis process, guiding further, more complex analyses and modeling.

Grouping and Aggregating Data in Pandas

GROUPING AND AGGREGATING data are powerful capabilities in Pandas that enable you to perform complex data analysis operations. These functionalities are particularly useful for summarizing data, understanding patterns, and making comparisons across different categories.

1. Grouping Data:

- Use the groupby() method to group data in a DataFrame based on one or more columns. This creates a GroupBy object which can be used for aggregation.

```
grouped = df.groupby('ColumnToGroupBy')
```

2. Aggregating Data:

- After grouping, you can apply aggregation methods to compute statistics for each group.

- Common aggregations include sum(), mean(), median(), count(), max(), and min().

```
mean_values = grouped.mean()

total_values = grouped.sum()
```

3. Aggregating Specific Columns:

- To aggregate only specific columns, select them after the groupby() method.

```
grouped['ColumnToAggregate'].sum()
```

4. Multiple Aggregations:

- Use agg() to perform multiple aggregation operations simultaneously.

```
grouped['ColumnToAggregate'].agg(['mean', 'sum', 'max'])
```

5. Grouping by Multiple Columns:

- You can group by multiple columns to get more granular insights.

```
grouped = df.groupby(['FirstColumnToGroupBy', 'SecondColumnToGroupBy'])
```

6. Resetting Index After Grouping:

- Aggregations often result in the grouped columns becoming the index of the resulting DataFrame. Use reset_index() to revert this.

```
result = grouped.mean().reset_index()
```

7. Custom Aggregation Functions:

- You can apply custom functions to groups using apply().

```
def custom_function(group):

return group.max() - group.min()

grouped['ColumnToAggregate'].apply(custom_function)
```

8. Pivot Tables:

- Pivot tables are another way to aggregate data, providing a spreadsheet-like layout.

df.pivot_table(values='ColumnToAggregate', index='RowIdentifier', columns='ColumnIdentifier', aggfunc='mean')

9. Exploring Grouped Data:

- Iterating over groups can be useful for more detailed analysis.

for name, group in grouped:

print(name)

print(group)

Grouping and aggregating data in Pandas are integral for analyzing subsets of data, identifying trends and patterns, and making data-driven decisions. These operations are highly flexible and can be tailored to specific analytical needs.

Pivot Tables and Cross Tabulations in Pandas

PIVOT TABLES AND CROSS tabulations are powerful tools in Pandas for summarizing and analyzing data. They help in reorganizing and aggregating datasets in a structured way, making them indispensable in data analysis.

Pivot Tables:

1. Creating Pivot Tables:

○ Use pivot_table() to create pivot tables. It allows you to define index/column values and aggregation functions.

pivot = df.pivot_table(values='ValueColumn', index='RowCategory', columns='ColumnCategory', aggfunc='mean')

○ In this example, the ValueColumn is aggregated (using the mean function), distributed across RowCategory and ColumnCategory.

2. Aggregation Functions:

○ You can use different aggregation functions like sum, mean, count, etc.

pivot = df.pivot_table(values='ValueColumn', index='RowCategory', aggfunc='sum')

3. Handling Missing Values:

○ Pivot tables automatically handle missing values by treating them as NaN. You can fill them using the fill_value parameter.

pivot = df.pivot_table(values='ValueColumn', index='RowCategory', fill_value=0)

4. Multiple Aggregations:

○ Pivot tables can also perform multiple aggregations.

```python
pivot = df.pivot_table(values='ValueColumn', index='RowCategory', aggfunc=['mean', 'sum'])
```

Cross Tabulations:

   1. **Creating Cross Tabulations:**

   ○ Cross tabulation (or crosstab) is used to compute a simple cross-tabulation of two (or more) factors. Use pd.crosstab() for this.

```python
crosstab = pd.crosstab(df['RowCategory'], df['ColumnCategory'])
```

   2. **Adding Margins:**

   ○ You can add row/column totals by setting the margins parameter to True.

```python
crosstab = pd.crosstab(df['RowCategory'], df['ColumnCategory'], margins=True)
```

   3. **Normalizing:**

   ○ Normalize the table to show proportions rather than counts by using the normalize parameter.

```python
crosstab = pd.crosstab(df['RowCategory'], df['ColumnCategory'], normalize='index')
```

   4. **Multiple Groups:**

   ○ Crosstab can be used to analyze the relationship between multiple categories.

```python
crosstab = pd.crosstab([df['FirstCategory'], df['SecondCategory']], df['ColumnCategory'])
```

Pivot tables and cross tabulations in Pandas provide a flexible and easy way to summarize and analyze your data. They are particularly useful for seeing the relationship between two or more variables and for breaking down the complexities of large datasets into simpler, understandable forms.

Time Series Analysis in Pandas

PANDAS IS PARTICULARLY strong in handling time series data, offering extensive capabilities for manipulating, analyzing, and visualizing temporal data. Here's an overview of how you can work with time series in Pandas:

1. Parsing Dates:

   ● When loading data, ensure that Pandas recognizes dates correctly using pd.to_datetime().

```python
df['date_column'] = pd.to_datetime(df['date_column'])
```

2. Setting the DateTimeIndex:

   ● It's often useful to set the date column as the DataFrame index.

df.set_index('date_column', inplace=True)

3. Time-based Indexing:

- Use date/time as indices to efficiently filter and select data.

df.loc['2020-01-01'] # Data on Jan 1, 2020

df.loc['2020-01':'2020-02'] # Data from January to February 2020

4. Resampling:

- Aggregate data over time intervals with resample(). For instance, converting from a higher frequency to a lower frequency (downsampling) like daily to monthly.

df.resample('M').mean() # Monthly averages

5. Rolling and Expanding Windows:

- Use rolling window calculations for moving averages or expanding windows for cumulative statistics.

df['column'].rolling(window=5).mean() # 5-day moving average

df['column'].expanding(min_periods=1).sum() # Cumulative sum

6. Shift and Difference:

- Use shift() and diff() for lagging and differencing time series data, which is useful for time-series forecasting models.

df['column'].shift(1) # Shift data by 1 period

df['column'].diff(1) # First difference of the data

7. Time Zone Handling:

- Convert time zones with tz_convert() for time series that involve data across multiple time zones.

df.index = df.index.tz_localize('UTC').tz_convert('America/New_York')

8. Period and Frequency Conversion:

- Convert time series frequency with asfreq() or to Periods with to_period().

df.asfreq('W', method='ffill') # Weekly frequency with forward fill

df.to_period('Q') # Convert to quarterly Periods

9. Plotting Time Series:

- Visualize time series data using Pandas' built-in plotting capabilities.

df['column'].plot()

10. Decomposition and Forecasting:

- While Pandas does not directly support time series decomposition or forecasting models, it integrates well with other libraries like statsmodels and scikit-learn that do.

Time series analysis in Pandas is a strong suit, thanks to its specialized date and time functions. These tools allow you to explore temporal patterns, trends, and relationships within your data, making Pandas a go-to library for any time series analysis task.

Full Example: Time Series Analysis with Pandas

Generating a Time Series

LET'S START BY GENERATING a time series dataset. Pandas makes this straightforward with its date_range function, which can produce a range of dates. Coupled with numpy, we can create a simulated time series data set for analysis.

import pandas as pd

import numpy as np

Create a date range: one year of daily data

date_range = pd.date_range(start='2023-01-01', end='2023-12-31', freq='D')

Generate random data to represent daily observations

data = np.random.randn(len(date_range))

time_series = pd.Series(data, index=date_range)

Time-based Indexing and Slicing

ONE OF THE STRENGTHS of Pandas is its ability to index and slice data easily, especially with time series data, enabling precise data extraction over specified intervals.

Extract data for March 2023

march_2023 = time_series['2023-03']

Resampling for Different Frequencies

RESAMPLING IS A METHOD to convert time series data from one frequency to another. This can help in summarizing or aggregating data over a specified period.

Compute the monthly mean of the daily data

monthly_mean = time_series.resample('M').mean()

Visualizing Time Series Data

VISUALIZATION PLAYS a critical role in the analysis of time series data. It helps in identifying trends, patterns, and anomalies.

import matplotlib.pyplot as plt

Plotting the daily and monthly mean time series data

plt.figure(figsize=(10, 6))

plt.plot(time_series, label='Daily')

plt.plot(monthly_mean, label='Monthly Mean', linewidth=3)

plt.title('Daily vs. Monthly Mean')

plt.xlabel('Date')

plt.ylabel('Value')

plt.legend()

plt.show()

Conclusion

THIS FULL EXAMPLE DEMONSTRATES the robust capabilities of Pandas for time series analysis, including generating, manipulating, resampling, and visualizing time series data. By leveraging Pandas along with other Python libraries like numpy and matplotlib, you can perform comprehensive time series analyses and gain deep insights into your data's temporal patterns and trends.

1. **Advanced Data Manipulation**
   Merging and Joining DataFrames in Pandas

Merging and joining are crucial operations in Pandas, enabling you to combine data from different sources into a single DataFrame. These operations are similar to SQL joins and are essential for data analysis involving multiple datasets.

1. Merge:

- merge() combines DataFrames based on common columns or indices.

merged_df = pd.merge(df1, df2, on='common_column')

- By default, it performs an inner join. You can specify different types of joins (left, right, outer, inner) using the how parameter.

pd.merge(df1, df2, on='common_column', how='left')

2. Join:

- join() is used for combining DataFrames based on their indices. It supports different join operations like merge().

joined_df = df1.join(df2, how='left')

3. Concatenation:

- concat() is used to append DataFrames either along the row axis or column axis.

concatenated_df = pd.concat([df1, df2], axis=0) # Row-wise concatenation

pd.concat([df1, df2], axis=1) # Column-wise concatenation

- It's useful for stacking similar DataFrames or for adding new rows/columns.

4. Handling Overlapping Data:

- When merging DataFrames with overlapping column names, Pandas automatically adds suffixes to them.

pd.merge(df1, df2, on='common_column', suffixes=('_left', '_right'))

5. Merging on Index:

- You can merge two DataFrames based on the index of one and the column of another.

pd.merge(df1, df2, left_index=True, right_on='matching_column')

6. Merge with Multiple Keys:

- Merge DataFrames based on multiple columns.

pd.merge(df1, df2, on=['common_column1', 'common_column2'])

7. Checking for Duplicate Keys:

- When merging, it's important to check for duplicate keys to avoid unexpected duplication in the resulting DataFrame.

if df1.duplicated(['key']).any() or df2.duplicated(['key']).any():

print("Warning: there are duplicate keys.")

Merging and joining are powerful techniques for data consolidation and analysis. They enable you to bring together data from different sources, aligning them into a unified structure for in-depth analysis and visualization. Understanding these operations is vital for effective data manipulation in Pandas.

Reshaping and Pivoting DataFrames in Pandas

RESHAPING AND PIVOTING are important techniques in Pandas, allowing you to reorganize your data for more effective analysis. These operations can transform the layout of your data, making it easier to understand and analyze.

1. Reshaping with stack and unstack:

stack() "compresses" a level in the DataFrame's columns to produce a Series.

stacked = df.stack()

unstack() does the opposite, "expanding" a level in the DataFrame's index to produce a DataFrame.

unstacked = stacked.unstack()

2. Pivot Tables:

Pivot tables allow you to reshape the DataFrame by specifying index/column values and an aggregation function.

pivot_table = df.pivot_table(values='Value', index='RowVariable', columns='ColumnVariable', aggfunc='mean')

3. melt:

melt() is used to transform or reshape data, turning columns into rows.

melted = df.melt(id_vars=['ID'], value_vars=['Variable1', 'Variable2'])

4. pivot:

Similar to pivot_table but used for reshaping data without aggregation.

pivoted = df.pivot(index='RowVariable', columns='ColumnVariable', values='Value')

5. wide_to_long:

This function helps reshape a DataFrame from wide format to long format.

pd.wide_to_long(df, stubnames='Var', i='ID', j='Year')

6. Cross Tabulations:

crosstab() is used to compute a cross-tabulation of two (or more) factors, which can help in reshaping the data for analysis.

pd.crosstab(df['RowFactor'], df['ColumnFactor'])

7. Reshaping by Indexing:

You can use set_index(), reset_index(), or reindex() to reshape data based on index manipulation.

df.set_index(['NewIndex'])

df.reset_index()

8. MultiIndex for Advanced Reshaping:

Pandas MultiIndex can be used for advanced reshaping. You can create hierarchical indexes at multiple levels for more complex reshaping.

df.set_index(['Level1', 'Level2'])

Reshaping and pivoting are essential tools for data preprocessing. They enable you to structure the data in a form that is suitable for specific types of analysis, improving both the efficiency and clarity of your data analysis processes.

Advanced Filtering Techniques in Pandas

ADVANCED FILTERING techniques in Pandas allow for more precise and complex data selection. These methods are crucial for working with large datasets or when specific conditions need to be met. Here are some advanced filtering techniques:

1. Boolean Indexing:

- Combine multiple conditions using bitwise operators (& for and, | for or).

filtered_df = df[(df['Age'] > 30) & (df['City'] == 'New York')]

2. Using query():

- The query() method allows you to filter using a query expression.

filtered_df = df.query('Age > 30 & City == "New York"')

3. Filtering with isin:

- The isin() method is useful for filtering data based on a list of values.

filtered_df = df[df['City'].isin(['New York', 'London'])]

4. Using where():

- The where() method is used to replace values that do not meet a condition, which is different from filtering out.

df_where = df.where(df['Age'] > 30)

5. Regular Expressions:

- For filtering strings, you can use regular expressions with the str accessor.

filtered_df = df[df['Name'].str.contains('^A', regex=True)]

6. Using filter():

- The filter() method is used for selecting columns based on their names.

```
filtered_df = df.filter(like='prefix')
```

7. Conditional Selection with np.where:

- Use np.where for more complex conditional logic. It's like an if-then-else statement for DataFrames.

```
import numpy as np

df['Category'] = np.where(df['Age'] > 30, 'Senior', 'Junior')
```

8. Index-based Selection:

- For complex index-based selection, use .loc[] and .iloc[].

```
filtered_df = df.loc[df['Age'] > 30, ['Name', 'Age']]
```

9. Using Functions with apply():

- Apply a custom function to filter data.

```
filtered_df = df[df['Age'].apply(lambda x: x > 30)]
```

10. Combining DataFrames for Filtering:

- Use methods like merge and join to combine DataFrames for complex filtering scenarios.

```
filtered_df = df.merge(filter_conditions_df, how='inner', on='KeyColumn')
```

These advanced techniques provide robust and flexible ways to filter data in Pandas, enabling you to handle a wide range of data filtering scenarios more effectively.

Working with Text Data in Pandas

PANDAS OFFERS A VARIETY of tools for efficiently working with text data. These functionalities are essential for cleaning, processing, and extracting insights from textual data within DataFrames. Here's how you can handle text data in Pandas:

1. String Operations with str:

- Pandas provides vectorized string functions, which can be accessed using the str accessor. These functions operate on each element of a column.

```
df['text_column'].str.upper() # Convert to uppercase

df['text_column'].str.len() # Calculate string length
```

2. Splitting Strings:

- Split strings into lists using str.split().

```
df['text_column'].str.split(' ')
```

3. Replacing Text:

- Use str.replace() to replace parts of a string.

```
df['text_column'].str.replace('old', 'new')
```

4. Extracting Substrings:

- Extract substrings using str.slice() or by using string indexing.

```
df['text_column'].str.slice(0, 5)
```

```
df['text_column'].str[0:5]
```

5. Regular Expressions:

- Use regular expressions for complex text manipulation and extraction.

```
df['text_column'].str.extract('(pattern)', expand=False)
```

```
df['text_column'].str.contains('pattern')
```

6. Removing Whitespace:

- Trim whitespace from strings.

```
df['text_column'].str.strip()
```

7. Handling Missing or Invalid Data:

- Manage missing or invalid text data.

```
df['text_column'].fillna('default_text')
```

```
df['text_column'].str.replace('NA', 'default_text')
```

8. Concatenating Strings:

- Combine strings from multiple columns.

```
df['new_column'] = df['text1'] + ' ' + df['text2']
```

9. Counting Occurrences:

- Count occurrences of a substring or pattern.

```
df['text_column'].str.count('pattern')
```

10. Working with Large Text Data:

● For large text datasets, consider applying operations in chunks or using Dask for parallel processing to improve performance.

Working with text data in Pandas efficiently requires leveraging these string methods, allowing you to clean, transform, and analyze textual data within DataFrames. These operations are particularly useful in natural language processing (NLP) tasks and when preparing data for machine learning mode

5. Data Visualization with Pandas

DATA VISUALIZATION is a crucial step in data analysis, offering an intuitive way to see and understand trends, outliers, and patterns in data. Pandas, integrated with Matplotlib, provides a simple yet powerful way to visualize data directly from DataFrames and Series.

Introduction to Data Visualization with Pandas:

1. **Why Visualize Data?**

○ Visualization helps in making sense of data, identifying trends, and conveying insights quickly and effectively.

○ It's easier to spot anomalies and patterns through visuals than by looking at raw numbers.

2. **Basic Plot Types:**

○ Pandas supports various plot types like line plots, bar plots, histograms, scatter plots, and more.

○ These plots can be created directly from Pandas objects.

3. **Line Plots:**

○ Ideal for showing trends over time. Use df.plot() or df.plot.line().

df['column'].plot()

4. **Bar Plots:**

○ Useful for comparing categorical data. Use df.plot.bar() for vertical bars or df.plot.barh() for horizontal bars.

df['categorical_column'].value_counts().plot.bar()

5. **Histograms:**

○ Great for showing distributions. Use df.plot.hist().

df['numerical_column'].plot.hist(bins=20)

6. **Scatter Plots:**

○ Ideal for showing the relationship between two numerical variables. Use df.plot.scatter().

df.plot.scatter(x='column1', y='column2')

7. Box Plots:

○ Useful for visualizing the distribution and variability of data. Use df.plot.box().

df.plot.box()

8. Customizing Plots:

○ Pandas plots can be customized by setting various parameters like title, xlabel, ylabel, figsize, and more.

○ You can further customize plots using Matplotlib functions.

9. Integration with Matplotlib:

○ While Pandas provides convenient wrappers for quick plotting, for more advanced visualizations, you can use Matplotlib directly.

○ Pandas DataFrames and Series can be passed as data sources to Matplotlib plot functions.

10. Saving Plots:

○ You can save plots to a file using plt.savefig().

import matplotlib.pyplot as plt

df.plot()

plt.savefig('output.png')

Data visualization with Pandas is a powerful way to communicate information and gain insights from data, making complex data more accessible and understandable. Whether you're exploring data, presenting findings, or building a data-driven story, effective visualization is key.

Plotting with Pandas

PANDAS SIMPLIFIES THE process of plotting data from DataFrames and Series, utilizing the capabilities of Matplotlib under the hood. Here's how you can create various types of plots using Pandas:

1. Line Plots:

● Line plots are default for DataFrame and Series plotting. They are suitable for showing trends over time.

df.plot() # Plots all columns against the index

df['column'].plot() # Plots a single column

2. Bar Plots:

- Bar plots are useful for comparing categorical data.

df['categorical_column'].value_counts().plot(kind='bar')

df.plot(kind='bar', stacked=True) # Stacked bar plot

3. Histograms:

- Histograms are great for showing the distribution of data.

df['numerical_column'].plot(kind='hist', bins=20)

4. Scatter Plots:

- Scatter plots are ideal for examining the relationship between two numerical variables.

df.plot(kind='scatter', x='column1', y='column2')

5. Box Plots:

- Box plots are used to show the distribution of data and identify outliers.

df.plot(kind='box')

6. Area Plots:

- Area plots are useful for comparing quantities and showing the composition over time.

df.plot(kind='area', stacked=False)

7. Pie Charts:

- Pie charts are best for showing proportions.

df['column'].plot(kind='pie', autopct='%1.1f%%')

8. Customizing Plots:

- Pandas plots can be customized by setting various parameters like title, xlabel, ylabel, figsize, color, etc.

df.plot(title='My Plot', figsize=(10, 6), color='red')

9. Combining Plots:

- You can combine multiple plots by using Matplotlib functions.

ax = df['column1'].plot()

df['column2'].plot(ax=ax)

plt.show()

10. Saving Plots: - Plots can be saved to a file using the savefig() function from Matplotlib. python import matplotlib.pyplot as plt df.plot() plt.savefig('plot.png')

Plotting with Pandas allows for a quick and efficient way to visualize your data and gain insights. Whether you are performing exploratory data analysis or preparing a report, these plotting capabilities are essential tools in your data analysis workflow.

Customizing Plots in Pandas

WHILE PANDAS PROVIDES a straightforward way to create plots, customizing them allows for more informative and visually appealing representations of data. Here's how you can customize plots in Pandas, using Matplotlib for finer control:

1. Basic Customizations:

- You can customize the size, title, labels, colors, and more directly in Pandas.

df.plot(figsize=(10, 6), title='My Custom Plot', color='green')

plt.xlabel('X-axis Label')

plt.ylabel('Y-axis Label')

2. Changing Plot Style:

- Matplotlib styles can be used to change the overall look of the plot.

plt.style.use('ggplot') # Use ggplot style

df.plot()

3. Customizing the Legend:

- Adjust legend position and styling.

df.plot()

plt.legend(loc='upper right', title='Legend Title')

4. Modifying Ticks:

- Ticks can be rotated and formatted for better readability.

df.plot()

plt.xticks(rotation=45)

plt.yticks(fontsize=10)

5. Adding Text and Annotations:

- Annotate specific points or add text to the plot.

df.plot()

plt.text(x=5, y=10, s='Important Point')

plt.annotate('Max Value', xy=(10, 20), xytext=(15, 25), arrowprops=dict(facecolor='black'))

6. Multiple Plots on Same Axes:

- Combine multiple plots for comparison.

df['column1'].plot()

df['column2'].plot(secondary_y=True) # Plot on a secondary Y-axis

7. Customizing Grids and Axes:

- Modify grid lines and axis limits.

df.plot()

plt.grid(True)

plt.xlim(0, 10)

plt.ylim(0, 100)

8. Using Different Plot Types:

- Mix different plot types for more effective visualizations.

df['column1'].plot(kind='bar')

df['column2'].plot(kind='line', color='red', secondary_y=True)

9. Handling Dates:

- When dealing with time series, you might want to format date ticks.

df.plot()

plt.gcf().autofmt_xdate() # Auto-format date on x-axis

10. Saving Customized Plots: - After customizing, save the plot using savefig(). python plt.savefig('customized_plot.png')

Customizing plots in Pandas using Matplotlib allows for a high degree of flexibility. You can tailor your visualizations to convey the right message more effectively and make them more accessible to your audience.

2. Real-World Projects and Case Studies

Project 1: Analyzing Financial Data

Objective: To perform an in-depth analysis of financial data, such as stock prices, trading volumes, or financial ratios, to uncover trends, assess risk, and make investment decisions.

Data Sources:

- Historical stock price and volume data from financial APIs like Yahoo Finance, Google Finance, or Quandl.

- Financial statements and ratios from company reports or financial databases.

Key Steps:

1. **Data Collection:**

○ Use APIs or web scraping to collect historical stock prices, trading volumes, and financial statement data.

○ Example: Retrieving data using yfinance in Python.

2. **Data Cleaning and Preparation:**

○ Handle missing values, outliers, and convert data types.

○ Normalize data if required, for instance, adjusting stock prices for splits or dividends.

3. **Exploratory Data Analysis (EDA):**

○ Visualize historical trends in stock prices and volumes.

○ Analyze summary statistics to understand the distribution of financial ratios.

○ Example: Plotting moving averages or calculating and visualizing return distributions.

4. **Performance Analysis:**

○ Calculate financial metrics like returns, volatility, and beta.

○ Compare the performance of different stocks or indices.

5. **Risk Analysis:**

○ Assess risk by calculating metrics such as Value at Risk (VaR) or Expected Shortfall.

○ Perform scenario analysis based on historical financial crises.

6. **Correlation Analysis:**

○ Analyze correlations between different stocks, sectors, or asset classes.

○ Identify diversification opportunities in a portfolio.

7. **Time-Series Analysis:**

○ Model stock price trends and volatility using time-series analysis (e.g., ARIMA, GARCH models).

8. **Predictive Modeling:**

○ Develop predictive models for stock prices or financial ratios using machine learning.

○ Backtest models to validate performance.

9. **Reporting and Visualization:**

○ Create dashboards and reports summarizing findings, trends, and recommendations.

○ Use data visualization techniques to present complex financial data in an accessible format.

10. **Conclusions and Recommendations:**

○ Provide insights on investment opportunities, risk management strategies, or areas for further research.

Tools and Libraries:

● Python with Pandas, NumPy, Matplotlib, Seaborn for data manipulation and visualization.

● Scikit-learn or TensorFlow for machine learning models.

● Specialized libraries like yfinance for data retrieval, statsmodels for statistical analysis, and plotly or dash for interactive visualizations.

Outcome: This project will equip you with a comprehensive understanding of financial data analysis, using real-world data to make informed investment decisions and risk assessments. The analytical skills and insights gained can be directly applied in finance roles or personal investment strategies.

In the next section we will have a hand on lab project on analyzing financial data, specifically focusing on stock market data. This project will involve collecting data, performing exploratory data analysis, computing financial metrics, and visualizing the results. I will include sample Python code snippets for each step.

Lab Project: Analyzing Stock Market Data

Objective:

Gain insights into stock market trends and performance by analyzing historical stock price data.

Tools and Libraries:

- Python
- Pandas for data manipulation
- NumPy for numerical calculations
- Matplotlib and Seaborn for visualization
- yfinance for fetching financial data

Project Steps:

1. Data Collection:

○ Use yfinance to fetch historical stock data.

```
IMPORT YFINANCE AS yf

stock = yf.Ticker("AAPL")

df = stock.history(period="1y") # Fetch 1 year of historical data
```

2. Data Exploration:

○ Examine the dataset for structure, missing values, and basic statistics.

```
print(df.head())

print(df.describe())
```

3. Data Cleaning:

○ Handle missing values, if any, or erroneous data points.

```
df.dropna(inplace=True) # Drop missing values
```

4. Exploratory Data Analysis (EDA):

○ Visualize stock price trends over time.

```python
import matplotlib.pyplot as plt

import seaborn as sns

sns.lineplot(data=df, x=df.index, y='Close')

plt.title('Stock Price Over Time')

plt.xlabel('Date')

plt.ylabel('Close Price')

plt.show()
```

5. **Calculating Daily Returns:**

   o Compute daily returns of the stock.

```python
df['Daily Return'] = df['Close'].pct_change()
```

6. **Volatility Analysis:**

   o Calculate and plot the rolling standard deviation of daily returns (volatility).

```python
df['Volatility'] = df['Daily Return'].rolling(window=20).std()

df['Volatility'].plot(title='Rolling 20-Day Volatility')

plt.show()
```

7. **Comparative Analysis:**

   o Compare with another stock or market index.

```python
sp500 = yf.Ticker("^GSPC").history(period="1y")

df['SP500'] = sp500['Close']

df[['Close', 'SP500']].plot()

plt.title('Stock vs. S&P 500')

plt.show()
```

8. **Correlation Analysis:**

   o Analyze the correlation between different stocks.

```python
df['MSFT'] = yf.Ticker("MSFT").history(period="1y")['Close']

correlation = df[['Close', 'SP500', 'MSFT']].corr()
```

```python
print(correlation)
```

9. Performance Metrics:

○ Calculate key financial metrics, e.g., annualized return, Sharpe ratio.

```python
annual_return = df['Daily Return'].mean() * 252

annual_volatility = df['Daily Return'].std() * (252**0.5)

sharpe_ratio = annual_return / annual_volatility

print(f"Annual Return: {annual_return}")

print(f"Sharpe Ratio: {sharpe_ratio}")
```

10. Conclusion:

○ Summarize key findings from the analysis, including risks, opportunities, and trends.

Outcome:

THIS PROJECT WILL PROVIDE practical experience in financial data analysis, encompassing data collection, manipulation, exploratory analysis, and visualization using Python. The skills and insights gained can be applied in investment analysis, portfolio management, or economic research.

This project is designed to be both educational and practical, offering a hands-on experience with real-world financial data. The Python code snippets provide a starting point for each step of the analysis.

Project 2: Data Analysis in Retail

Objective:

To analyze retail data for insights into sales trends, customer behavior, and inventory management, which can help in making informed business decisions.

Tools and Libraries:

- Python

- Pandas for data manipulation

- Matplotlib and Seaborn for visualization

- Scikit-learn for any predictive modeling

Dataset:

A RETAIL DATASET, WHICH can be a real-world dataset from a company or a publicly available dataset like the UCI Machine Learning Repository's "Online Retail" dataset.

Project Steps:

1. **Data Collection:**

○ Obtain a retail dataset. If using the UCI dataset, it can be downloaded directly.

IMPORT PANDAS AS PD

df = pd.read_excel('Online Retail.xlsx')

2. **Data Cleaning:**

○ Handle missing values, duplicate records, and correct data types.

df.dropna(inplace=True)

df['InvoiceDate'] = pd.to_datetime(df['InvoiceDate'])

3. **Exploratory Data Analysis (EDA):**

○ Analyze the data for sales trends, popular products, and customer purchase patterns.

df['TotalPrice'] = df['Quantity'] * df['UnitPrice']

```
df.groupby(df['InvoiceDate'].dt.date)['TotalPrice'].sum().plot()
```

4. Customer Segmentation:

○ Segment customers based on purchase history using RFM (Recency, Frequency, Monetary) analysis.

```
# Assuming the analysis is done at a later date, say '2021-01-01'

import datetime as dt

NOW = dt.datetime(2021,1,1)

rfmTable = df.groupby('CustomerID').agg({'InvoiceDate': lambda x: (NOW - x.max()).days, 'InvoiceNo': lambda x: len(x), 'TotalPrice': lambda x: x.sum()})
```

5. Market Basket Analysis:

○ Use association rule mining to find products that are frequently bought together.

○ Python's mlxtend library can be used for this analysis.

6. Inventory Management:

○ Analyze inventory levels, identify fast and slow-moving products.

○ Predict stock requirements using time-series forecasting or regression models.

7. Sales Prediction:

○ Build predictive models to forecast future sales.

○ Use regression models, time series analysis, or machine learning methods.

8. Customer Satisfaction Analysis:

○ Analyze customer reviews or ratings if available.

○ Use sentiment analysis to gauge customer satisfaction.

9. Data Visualization:

○ Create interactive dashboards for real-time monitoring of key metrics.

○ Use libraries like Plotly or Dash for advanced visualizations.

10. Reporting and Insights:

○ Prepare a comprehensive report of the findings with actionable insights.

○ Recommendations on inventory management, marketing strategies, and customer relationship management.

Outcome:

THIS PROJECT WILL PROVIDE practical experience in handling retail data, performing a variety of analyses to extract meaningful insights. The skills gained are directly applicable in retail analytics roles, aiding in data-driven decision-making.

This project covers a broad range of analyses pertinent to the retail industry, providing a holistic view of how data analytics can be leveraged in a retail context. The Python snippets offer a foundation for each analytical step.

The next section is an outline a comprehensive lab project focusing on retail data analysis. This project will involve various steps, from data collection to advanced analysis, and visualization. I will include Python code snippets for key tasks.

Lab Project: Retail Data Analysis

Objective:

To analyze retail data to gain insights into sales performance, customer behavior, and inventory management.

Tools and Libraries:

- Python

- Pandas for data manipulation

- Matplotlib and Seaborn for visualization

- Scikit-learn for predictive modeling (if needed)

Dataset:

A RETAIL DATASET, SUCH as the "Online Retail" dataset from the UCI Machine Learning Repository.

Project Steps:

1. **Data Collection:**

   ○ Load the dataset.

IMPORT PANDAS AS PD

df = pd.read_csv('online_retail.csv')

2. **Data Cleaning and Preparation:**

   ○ Handle missing values and data inconsistencies.

df.dropna(subset=['CustomerID'], inplace=True)

df['InvoiceDate'] = pd.to_datetime(df['InvoiceDate'])

3. **Exploratory Data Analysis (EDA):**

   ○ Perform an initial analysis to understand the dataset.

import matplotlib.pyplot as plt

df['TotalPrice'] = df['Quantity'] * df['UnitPrice']

```python
df.groupby(df['InvoiceDate'].dt.month)['TotalPrice'].sum().plot(kind='bar')

plt.title('Monthly Sales')

plt.xlabel('Month')

plt.ylabel('Total Sales')

plt.show()
```

4. **Customer Segmentation (RFM Analysis):**

   ○ Segment customers using RFM analysis.

```python
latest_date = df['InvoiceDate'].max() + pd.DateOffset(days=1)

rfm_df = df.groupby('CustomerID').agg({'InvoiceDate': lambda x: (latest_date - x.max()).days,

'InvoiceNo': 'count',

'TotalPrice': 'sum'})

rfm_df.rename(columns={'InvoiceDate': 'Recency', 'InvoiceNo': 'Frequency', 'TotalPrice': 'MonetaryValue'},
inplace=True)
```

5. **Product Analysis:**

   ○ Analyze the most sold and most profitable products.

```python
top_products = df.groupby('Description').agg(TotalSales=('TotalPrice', 'sum'),

TotalQuantity=('Quantity', 'sum')).nlargest(10, 'TotalSales')
```

6. **Time Series Analysis:**

   ○ Perform time-series analysis for sales forecasting.

```python
# Example: Monthly resampling

monthly_sales = df.set_index('InvoiceDate')['TotalPrice'].resample('M').sum()

monthly_sales.plot()

plt.title('Monthly Sales Over Time')

plt.show()
```

7. **Predictive Modeling:**

   ○ If required, build a predictive model for sales or customer behavior.

   ○ Example: Linear regression, decision trees, or any other suitable model.

8. Visualizing Data:

○ Create insightful visualizations.

```
import seaborn as sns

sns.heatmap(rfm_df.corr(), annot=True)

plt.show()
```

9. Actionable Insights and Recommendations:

○ Based on the analysis, provide insights and business recommendations.

Outcome:

THIS PROJECT WILL LEAD to a better understanding of retail dynamics, customer behavior, and sales trends. It will provide actionable insights for optimizing sales strategies and improving customer engagement.

This lab project is designed to offer a comprehensive experience in retail data analysis, leveraging Python and its libraries. The code snippets provide a framework that can be expanded with more advanced analyses and customized visualizations based on specific project requirements.

Project 3: Time Series Forecasting

Objective:

To develop a time series forecasting model to predict future trends, which is crucial for businesses in planning and decision-making. This project could focus on forecasting sales, stock prices, weather patterns, etc.

Tools and Libraries:

- Python

- Pandas for data manipulation

- Matplotlib and Seaborn for visualization

- Statsmodels or scikit-learn for time series modeling

- Optionally, libraries like Prophet for advanced forecasting

Dataset:

DEPENDING ON THE FOCUS, use an appropriate time series dataset like historical sales data, stock market data, or weather data. These can be sourced from public datasets or APIs.

Project Steps:

1. **Data Collection:**

○ Load the dataset. For example, if using stock data:

IMPORT YFINANCE AS yf

data = yf.download('AAPL', start='2015-01-01', end='2021-01-01')

2. **Data Preparation:**

○ Process and clean the data as necessary.

data.dropna(inplace=True)

data = data['Close'] # Focus on the closing price for simplicity

3. **Exploratory Data Analysis:**

○ Perform an initial analysis to understand patterns, trends, and seasonality.

```
data.plot()

plt.title('Stock Price Over Time')

plt.show()
```

4. **Decomposing Time Series:**

○ Decompose the time series to observe its components.

```
from statsmodels.tsa.seasonal import seasonal_decompose

decomposition = seasonal_decompose(data, model='multiplicative')

decomposition.plot()

plt.show()
```

5. **Time Series Stationarity:**

○ Test for stationarity and apply transformations if necessary.

```
from statsmodels.tsa.stattools import adfuller

result = adfuller(data)

print('ADF Statistic: %f' % result[0])
```

6. **Building a Forecasting Model:**

○ Develop a forecasting model using techniques like ARIMA, SARIMA, or LSTM.

```
from statsmodels.tsa.arima.model import ARIMA

model = ARIMA(data, order=(5,1,0))

model_fit = model.fit()
```

7. **Model Evaluation:**

○ Evaluate the model using metrics like RMSE and perform cross-validation.

```
from sklearn.metrics import mean_squared_error

predictions = model_fit.forecast(steps=365)

mse = mean_squared_error(data[-365:], predictions)
```

8. **Future Predictions:**

○ Use the model to make future predictions.

```python
future_forecast = model_fit.forecast(steps=365)
```

```python
future_forecast.plot()
```

9. **Visualization and Reporting:**

   ○ Visualize the forecasting results and prepare a report.

```python
plt.plot(data, label='Historical')
```

```python
plt.plot(future_forecast, label='Forecast')
```

```python
plt.title('Time Series Forecast')
```

```python
plt.legend()
```

```python
plt.show()
```

10. **Actionable Insights:**

    ○ Provide insights and implications of the forecast for business decisions.

Outcome:

THIS PROJECT WILL DELIVER a predictive model for time series data, offering insights into future trends. It's particularly valuable in sectors where forecasting is essential, such as finance, supply chain, and weather prediction.

This lab project covers essential steps in time series analysis and forecasting, providing a practical framework that can be applied to various real-world scenarios. The Python code snippets serve as a starting point for each stage of the analysis.

Certainly! Let's outline a comprehensive lab project on time series forecasting. This project will be detailed, including data preparation, analysis, model development, evaluation, and visualization, complete with Python code snippets.

Lab Project: Time Series Forecasting

Objective:

Develop a time series model to forecast future values based on historical data, applicable to domains like finance, weather, sales, etc.

Tools and Libraries:

- Python

- Pandas for data manipulation

- Matplotlib for visualization

- Statsmodels for time series modeling

Dataset:

WE'LL USE STOCK PRICE data for this project, but the approach can be adapted to other time series data.

Project Steps:

1. Data Collection:

○ Fetch historical stock data using yfinance.

IMPORT YFINANCE AS yf

data = yf.download('AAPL', start='2010-01-01', end='2020-12-31')['Close']

2. Data Preparation:

○ Ensure no missing values and index is a datetime.

data = data.asfreq('b') # 'b' for business day frequency

data.fillna(method='ffill', inplace=True) # Forward fill missing values

3. Exploratory Data Analysis:

○ Visualize the data to understand patterns.

import matplotlib.pyplot as plt

data.plot()

```python
plt.title('AAPL Stock Closing Prices')

plt.show()
```

4. **Testing for Stationarity:**

   o Use Augmented Dickey-Fuller test.

```python
from statsmodels.tsa.stattools import adfuller

result = adfuller(data)

print('ADF Statistic:', result[0])

print('p-value:', result[1])
```

5. **Differencing (if needed):**

   o If data is not stationary, apply differencing.

```python
data_diff = data.diff().dropna()
```

6. **ARIMA Model Development:**

   o Develop an ARIMA model for forecasting.

```python
from statsmodels.tsa.arima.model import ARIMA

model = ARIMA(data_diff, order=(5,1,0))

model_fit = model.fit()
```

7. **Model Diagnostics:**

   o Check residuals and model fit.

```python
model_fit.plot_diagnostics(figsize=(10, 8))

plt.show()
```

8. **Forecasting:**

   o Forecast future values.

```python
forecast = model_fit.forecast(steps=30) # Forecast next 30 days

forecast.plot()

plt.title('30 Day Forecast')

plt.show()
```

9. Evaluating the Model:

○ Split data into train and test sets to evaluate model performance.

train = data[:'2019']

test = data['2020']

model = ARIMA(train, order=(5,1,0))

model_fit = model.fit()

predictions = model_fit.forecast(steps=len(test))

plt.plot(test.index, predictions, color='red', label='Predictions')

plt.plot(test, label='Actual')

plt.legend()

plt.show()

10. Conclusion and Insights:

○ Analyze the results, providing insights and potential improvements.

Outcome:

THIS PROJECT WILL DEMONSTRATE the application of time series analysis and forecasting techniques using Python, delivering a model that can predict future stock prices. The skills acquired can be applied to various forecasting problems.

This project provides hands-on experience with time series forecasting, covering all the essential steps from data preparation to model evaluation. The Python code snippets serve as practical examples for each stage of the project.

3 . Performance Tuning and Scaling Pandas

● Optimizing Pandas Code

Performance Tuning and Scaling Pandas

Optimizing Pandas code is crucial when dealing with large datasets or computationally intensive data processing tasks. Efficient use of Pandas not only speeds up computations but also ensures better resource utilization. Here are key strategies for optimizing Pandas code:

1. Using Efficient Data Types:

- Opt for more efficient data types to reduce memory usage. For instance, use category type for categorical data and smaller numeric types like int32, float32 when possible.

DF['CATEGORY_COLUMN'] = df['category_column'].astype('category')

df['integer_column'] = df['integer_column'].astype('int32')

2. Selecting Columns Wisely:

- When performing operations, select only the necessary columns to reduce computation time and memory usage.

DF_SUBSET = DF[['NEEDED_column1', 'needed_column2']]

3. Vectorized Operations:

- Use Pandas' vectorized operations instead of applying functions row-wise, as they are more efficient.

DF['NEW_COLUMN'] = df['column1'] * df['column2']

4. Avoiding Loops:

- Avoid using loops, especially for loops. Opt for Pandas methods like apply(), map(), or vectorized operations.

DF['PROCESSED_COLUMN'] = df['text_column'].apply(lambda x: x.lower())

5. Using Efficient Functions:

- Use efficient Pandas functions like groupby() and merge() wisely. Be mindful of using groupby() with large number of groups.

6. Incremental Processing:

- For extremely large datasets, consider processing data incrementally or in chunks.

```
CHUNK_SIZE = 10000

for chunk in pd.read_csv('large_file.csv', chunksize=chunk_size):

process(chunk)
```

7. Indexing:

- Set appropriate indices for quicker data retrievals, especially when performing merging and slicing operations.

```
DF.SET_INDEX('ID_COLUMN', inplace=True)
```

8. Parallel Processing:

- For computationally intensive tasks, consider using parallel processing frameworks like Dask or multiprocessing.

9. Memory Management:

- Regularly delete objects that are no longer needed and use gc.collect() to free up memory.

10. Query Optimization:

- For complex queries, break them into multiple steps and use temporary variables. This can be more efficient than a single complex query.

11. Profiling Code:

- Profile your Pandas code to find bottlenecks using Python's cProfile module or Pandas' memory_usage() method.

12. Updating Pandas:

- Ensure you're using the latest version of Pandas, as each new release often includes performance improvements.

BY IMPLEMENTING THESE strategies, you can significantly enhance the performance of your Pandas code, making it well-suited for handling large datasets and complex data processing tasks.

Working with Large Datasets in Pandas

Handling large datasets in Pandas requires specific strategies to ensure efficient processing and memory management. Here are some techniques and best practices for working with large datasets:

1. Efficient Data Loading:

SPECIFY DATA TYPES: When loading data, specify exact data types to reduce memory usage.

dtypes = {'column1': 'int32', 'column2': 'float32'}

df = pd.read_csv('large_file.csv', dtype=dtypes)

Use Columns Wisely: Load only the necessary columns.

df = pd.read_csv('large_file.csv', usecols=['needed_column1', 'needed_column2'])

2. Chunk Processing:

PROCESS DATA IN CHUNKS rather than loading the entire dataset into memory.

chunk_size = 10000 # Adjust the size based on your memory

for chunk in pd.read_csv('large_file.csv', chunksize=chunk_size):

process(chunk)

3. Optimize Memory:

CONVERT DATA TYPES: After loading, convert data types to more memory-efficient formats where possible.

df['column'] = pd.to_numeric(df['column'], downcast='float')

Use Categoricals: For string columns with repeated values, convert them to categorical data.

df['category_column'] = df['category_column'].astype('category')

4. Filtering Data:

FILTER OUT UNNECESSARY data as early as possible to reduce the dataset size.

df = df[df['filter_column'] > value]

5. Efficient Aggregations and Operations:

- Use vectorized operations and efficient aggregations.

- Avoid looping through DataFrame rows. Use apply(), groupby(), or vectorized functions.

6. Using Dask for Parallel Computing:

FOR DATASETS THAT ARE too large for memory, use Dask, a parallel computing library that integrates with Pandas.

import dask.dataframe as dd

ddf = dd.read_csv('large_file.csv')

7. Incremental Loading and Processing:

- If working with SQL databases, consider loading and processing data incrementally.

8. Sampling Data:

FOR EXPLORATORY ANALYSIS, work with a sample of your large dataset.

df_sample = df.sample(frac=0.1) # Adjust the fraction based on your needs

9. Utilizing Efficient Storage Formats:

STORE AND LOAD DATA in efficient formats like Parquet, which is optimized for size and speed.

df.to_parquet('data.parquet')

df = pd.read_parquet('data.parquet')

10. Cleaning Up:

REGULARLY DELETE VARIABLES that are no longer needed and use Python's garbage collection to free up memory.

import gc

del unused_variable

gc.collect()

By following these practices, you can effectively manage and analyze large datasets in Pandas, minimizing memory usage and improving processing efficiency.

Integration with Dask for Parallel Computing in Pandas

When working with extremely large datasets that exceed your machine's memory capacity, integrating Pandas with Dask can be a game-changer. Dask is a parallel computing library that seamlessly scales Pandas' data processing capabilities. It allows you to work with large datasets efficiently by breaking them into smaller, manageable chunks and processing these chunks in parallel.

How Dask Works with Pandas:

1. **Lazy Evaluation:**

○ Dask operates on a principle of lazy evaluation. Computations are not performed immediately but are executed in parallel when you specifically ask for the results.

2. **Dask DataFrame:**

○ A Dask DataFrame is a large parallel DataFrame composed of many smaller Pandas DataFrames, split along the index. These DataFrames are computed on different threads or processes.

Basic Integration:

INSTALL DASK:

pip install dask

1.

   2. **Create a Dask DataFrame:**

○ Import Dask and read a file as a Dask DataFrame.

import dask.dataframe as dd

ddf = dd.read_csv('large_dataset.csv')

   3.

Operations with Dask:

1. **Performing Operations:**

○ Operations on a Dask DataFrame are similar to Pandas but executed in parallel.

RESULT = DDF.GROUPBY('column').sum()

2. Computing Results:

○ Call .compute() to perform the computation and get the result as a Pandas DataFrame.

computed_df = result.compute()

3. Handling Larger-than-memory Data:

○ Dask can handle datasets larger than your machine's RAM by breaking the data into chunks and only loading chunks into memory as needed.

4. Parallel Processing:

○ Dask automatically utilizes all available CPU cores for parallel processing, significantly speeding up computations on large datasets.

Combining Pandas and Dask:

1. Converting Between Dask and Pandas:

○ Convert a Pandas DataFrame to a Dask DataFrame.

DDF = DD.FROM_PANDAS(pandas_df, npartitions=10)

○ Convert a Dask DataFrame to a Pandas DataFrame.

pandas_df = ddf.compute()

2. Using Dask for Heavy Computations:

○ Perform heavy data processing tasks with Dask and switch back to Pandas for fine-tuned analysis and visualization.

Considerations:

● **Memory Management:** Be mindful of the size of data being computed at any time to avoid memory overflow.

● **Computation Time:** While Dask accelerates computation, especially for large datasets, it can add overhead for smaller datasets. It's optimal for large-scale data processing.

● **Compatibility:** Most Pandas operations are available in Dask, but there might be some limitations or slight differences in behavior.

BY LEVERAGING DASK for parallel computing, you can scale your Pandas workflows to handle very large datasets efficiently, utilizing the power of distributed computing.

1. Best Practices and Tips

○ Writing Efficient Pandas Code

2. Best Practices and Tips for Writing Efficient Pandas Code

Writing efficient code in Pandas is key to handling data effectively, especially when working with large datasets. Here are several best practices and tips:

1. Use Vectorized Operations:

PANDAS IS OPTIMIZED for vectorized operations. Using built-in functions instead of applying operations via loops can significantly enhance performance.

```
df['new_column'] = df['column1'] + df['column2']
```

2. Avoid Loops When Possible:

LOOPS, ESPECIALLY FOR loops, are slow. Opt for Pandas' apply(), map(), or other vectorized functions.

```
df['processed_column'] = df['text_column'].apply(lambda x: x.upper())
```

3. Use Efficient Data Types:

CONVERTING COLUMNS to more efficient data types can reduce memory usage. For instance, changing float64 to float32 or converting string columns to categorical when there are few unique values.

```
df['category_column'] = df['category_column'].astype('category')
```

4. Select Data Efficiently:

ONLY SELECT THE COLUMNS or rows needed for your analysis. This reduces memory usage and speeds up computations.

```
df_subset = df[['needed_column1', 'needed_column2']]
```

5. Use chunksize for Large Files:

WHEN READING LARGE files, use the chunksize parameter in read_csv() to process the file in chunks.

```
iterator = pd.read_csv('large_file.csv', chunksize=1000)

for chunk in iterator:

process(chunk)
```

6. Avoid Chained Indexing:

CHAINED INDEXING (LIKE df['column']['row']) can lead to inefficiencies and unexpected results. Use loc or iloc instead.

df.loc[row_index, 'column']

7. Use In-Place Operations:

WHERE APPROPRIATE, use the inplace=True parameter to avoid creating copies of the data.

df.dropna(inplace=True)

8. Use cat Accessor for Categorical Data:

FOR CATEGORICAL DATA, use the cat accessor for efficient processing.

df['category_column'].cat.codes

9. Exploit Pandas Functions:

- Utilize Pandas' extensive functions and methods, like groupby, merge, and pivot_table, which are optimized for performance.

10. Profile Your Code:

USE PROFILING TOOLS to identify bottlenecks. Python's built-in cProfile or Pandas' memory_usage() can be useful.

import cProfile

cProfile.run('df.apply(func)')

11. Keep Pandas Updated:

- Use the latest version of Pandas, as each update often includes performance improvements and bug fixes.

12. Consider Parallel Processing for Large Scale Data:

- For very large datasets, consider using libraries like Dask or Ray to parallelize operations.

BY FOLLOWING THESE best practices, you can write more efficient and effective Pandas code, which is especially important when working with large or complex datasets.

Common Pitfalls in Pandas and How to Avoid Them

Working with Pandas is incredibly powerful, but there are common pitfalls that can lead to errors or inefficient code. Here's a list of some typical issues and how to avoid them:

1. Inefficient Loops:

- **Pitfall:** Using loops to iterate over DataFrames.

- **Solution:** Utilize vectorized operations and Pandas' apply(), map(), or groupby() functions for efficient computations.

2. Chained Assignment:

- **Pitfall:** Chained assignments like df[a][b] = value can lead to unpredictable results due to Pandas' "chained indexing."

- **Solution:** Use loc or iloc for assignments: df.loc[a, b] = value.

3. Ignoring Data Types:

- **Pitfall:** Overlooking the data type of columns, leading to increased memory usage and slower computations.

- **Solution:** Convert columns to appropriate data types (e.g., category, int32, float32) and use memory_usage() to monitor memory consumption.

4. Incorrect Aggregation or Grouping:

- **Pitfall:** Misapplying groupby leading to incorrect aggregations.

- **Solution:** Clearly understand how groupby works, especially the difference between groupby().agg() and groupby().transform().

5. Not Handling Missing Data:

- **Pitfall:** Ignoring missing or NaN values in data, potentially skewing results.

- **Solution:** Use methods like isna(), fillna(), dropna() to handle missing data appropriately.

6. In-place Modifications:

- **Pitfall:** Overusing the inplace=True parameter without understanding its impact.

- **Solution:** Be cautious with inplace changes. They can save memory but make the code less readable and debuggable.

7. Ignoring Index Alignment:

- **Pitfall:** Forgetting that operations align on indices, leading to unexpected results.

- **Solution:** Be aware of index alignment in operations, especially when working with multiple DataFrames or Series.

8. Not Utilizing Datetime Functions:

- **Pitfall:** Manually parsing and manipulating datetime data.

- **Solution:** Use Pandas' built-in datetime functionalities for efficient parsing and manipulation.

9. Ignoring Read/Write Options:

- **Pitfall:** Using default read/write methods without tuning them for performance or data format.

- **Solution:** Customize parameters in read_csv(), to_csv(), etc., to match your data format and optimize performance.

10. Overlooking Vectorized String Methods:

- **Pitfall:** Looping over strings in a DataFrame for text manipulation.

- **Solution:** Use Pandas' vectorized string methods under str accessor for efficient text processing.

11. Not Checking for Duplicate Data:

- **Pitfall:** Neglecting the presence of duplicate entries in your dataset.

- **Solution:** Use drop_duplicates() or duplicated() to identify and handle duplicates.

12. Failing to Profile the Code:

- **Pitfall:** Not profiling code and thus missing out on identifying bottlenecks.

- **Solution:** Regularly use profiling tools to identify slow sections of your code.

BY BEING AWARE OF THESE common pitfalls and knowing how to avoid them, you can make your Pandas code more efficient, reliable, and maintainable.

Resources for Further Learning in Pandas

Expanding your knowledge and skills in Pandas is a continuous process. Here are some valuable resources for further learning, ranging from beginner to advanced levels:

1. Official Pandas Documentation:

- **Description:** Comprehensive and a must-read for understanding the basics to advanced functionalities of Pandas.

- **Link:** Pandas Documentation[1]

2. Books:

- **"Python for Data Analysis" by Wes McKinney:**

  ○ **Description:** Written by the creator of Pandas, this book is great for beginners and intermediates.

- **"Pandas Cookbook" by Theodore Petrou:**

  ○ **Description:** Offers practical recipes for complex data manipulation tasks.

3. Online Courses:

- **Coursera and Udemy:**

  ○ **Description:** These platforms offer various courses on Pandas, often part of larger data science specializations.

- **DataCamp:**

  ○ **Description:** DataCamp provides interactive courses specifically focused on Pandas and data manipulation.

4. Interactive Platforms:

- **Kaggle:**

  ○ **Description:** Kaggle offers Pandas-based challenges and datasets to practice real-world data analysis.

- **LeetCode:**

  ○ **Description:** Offers programming challenges that include data manipulation tasks.

---

1. https://pandas.pydata.org/pandas-docs/stable/

5. Tutorials and Blogs:

- **Towards Data Science on Medium:**

  ○ **Description:** A wealth of articles and tutorials from various authors.

- **Real Python:**

  ○ **Description:** Provides tutorials and guides, great for both beginners and experienced users.

6. YouTube Channels:

- **Corey Schafer, Data School:**

  ○ **Description:** These channels have detailed and beginner-friendly video tutorials on Pandas and data analysis.

7. Community and Forums:

- **Stack Overflow:**

  ○ **Description:** Great for getting answers to specific questions or problems you're facing.

- **Reddit (r/datascience, r/learnpython):**

  ○ **Description:** Active communities for sharing resources and solving queries.

8. GitHub Repositories:

- **Description:** Explore repositories that use Pandas for data analysis projects. They can provide real-world code examples and use cases.

9. Podcasts:

- **Talk Python To Me, Python Bytes:**

  ○ **Description:** These podcasts occasionally cover Pandas and data analysis topics.

10. Meetups and Conferences:

- **PyCon, PyData:**

  ○ **Description:** Attending these conferences (virtually or in-person) can provide insights into the latest trends and best practices.

11. Jupyter Notebooks:

- **Description:** Exploring Jupyter Notebooks shared by others can be a great way to see Pandas in action.

CONTINUOUSLY EXPLORING these resources will help you stay updated with the latest tools and techniques in Pandas, enhancing your data analysis skills. Remember, the key to mastering Pandas is consistent practice and experimentation with real datasets.

Appendix: Glossary of Terms in Pandas and Data Analysis

Understanding the terminology is crucial in working with Pandas and data analysis. Here's a glossary of some common terms you'll encounter:

1. DataFrame:

- A two-dimensional, size-mutable, and potentially heterogeneous tabular data structure with labeled axes (rows and columns). Think of it like a spreadsheet or SQL table in memory.

2. Series:

- A one-dimensional labeled array capable of holding any data type. Essentially, it's a single column from a DataFrame.

3. Index:

- The 'row labels' of the DataFrame or Series. It's like an address, that's how any data point across the DataFrame or Series can be accessed.

4. NaN:

- Stands for 'Not a Number'; it's Pandas' default missing value marker.

5. Vectorization:

- The process of applying operations to entire arrays instead of individual elements, which boosts performance and speed.

6. GroupBy:

- A process involving one or more of the following steps: Splitting the data into groups based on some criteria, applying a function to each group independently, and combining the results into a data structure.

7. Merge/Join:

- Combining DataFrames based on common keys/columns, similar to SQL join operations.

8. Concatenation:

- Joining two or more DataFrames along an axis.

9. Dtype:

- The data type of a Series/Column in a DataFrame, such as float, int, bool, datetime64[ns], and object.

10. Resampling:

- A method used to convert time series data from one frequency to another (e.g., converting seconds data into 5-minutes data).

11. Pivot Table:

- A data summarization tool that's often used in data processing to create a more convenient table format.

12. Apply Function:

- Used to apply a function along an axis of the DataFrame or on a Series.

13. Lambda Function:

- An anonymous function in Python, often used in combination with apply() and other such methods.

14. Cross Tabulation:

- A method to quantitatively analyze the relationship between multiple variables.

15. ARIMA/SARIMA:

- AutoRegressive Integrated Moving Average, a popular statistical method for time series forecasting.

16. Correlation:

- A statistical measure that expresses the extent to which two variables are linearly related.

17. Outlier:

- A data point that differs significantly from other observations, potentially indicating a measurement or data entry error.

THIS GLOSSARY COVERS fundamental terms that are frequently used in Pandas and general data analysis. Familiarity with these terms will enhance your understanding and ability to effectively utilize Pandas for data manipulation and analysis.

References and Further Reading for Pandas and Data Analysis

―――――

Expanding your understanding of Pandas and data analysis involves diving into a range of resources. Below is a list of references and materials for further reading that can deepen your knowledge:

Books:

1. **"Python for Data Analysis" by Wes McKinney:**

○ An excellent resource for beginners to advanced users, covering Pandas and data analysis techniques.

2. **"Pandas Cookbook" by Theodore Petrou:**

○ Offers practical recipes and solutions for complex data manipulation tasks.

3. **"Data Science Handbook" by Jake VanderPlas:**

○ Provides a broader view of data science with Python, including useful Pandas applications.

4. **"Hands-On Data Analysis with NumPy and Pandas" by Curtis Miller:**

○ Focuses on practical data analysis tasks, offering a hands-on approach.

Online Documentation and Tutorials:

1. **Pandas Official Documentation:**

○ Pandas Documentation[1]

○ The definitive guide and reference to all Pandas functionalities.

2. **Real Python Tutorials:**

○ Real Python[2]

○ Offers a range of tutorials from basic to advanced levels, specifically on Python and Pandas.

3. **Towards Data Science Blog:**

○ A Medium publication with numerous articles and tutorials on Pandas and data analysis.

---

1. https://pandas.pydata.org/pandas-docs/stable/

2. https://realpython.com/

Online Courses:

1. **Coursera and Udemy Courses:**

○ These platforms have various comprehensive courses on Pandas and Python for data analysis.

2. **DataCamp's Pandas Courses:**

○ Interactive courses focusing on practical aspects of using Pandas in data science.

Video Tutorials:

1. **Corey Schafer's Python Pandas Tutorial on YouTube:**

○ Provides a great beginner-friendly video series on Pandas.

2. **Data School YouTube Channel:**

○ Offers in-depth tutorials on specific Pandas functionalities.

Forums and Community:

1. **Stack Overflow:**

○ A rich community for asking questions and finding answers to specific coding issues in Pandas.

2. **Pandas Tag in Stack Overflow:**

○ Direct link: Pandas Questions - Stack Overflow[3]

3. **Reddit's r/learnpython and r/datascience:**

○ Active communities where you can discuss Python and Pandas related topics.

Research Papers and Articles:

1. **Google Scholar:**

○ Searching for "Pandas Python" or "data analysis with Python" can yield academic papers and advanced studies.

2. **Journals like JSS (Journal of Statistical Software) and JMLR (Journal of Machine Learning Research):**

○ Often contain advanced topics and case studies involving Pandas and data analysis.

---

3. https://stackoverflow.com/questions/tagged/pandas

THESE RESOURCES COLLECTIVELY provide a comprehensive learning path, from foundational concepts to advanced applications of Pandas in various data analysis scenarios. Whether you prefer books, interactive courses, community discussions, or academic papers, there's a wealth of information available to enhance your Pandas skills and knowledge.

Index

The index below organizes the key topics and concepts covered in the Pandas course book. Each entry is associated with the section where the topic is discussed in detail.

1. **Introduction to Pandas**

○ Overview of Pandas

○ Importance in Data Analysis

○ Setting up the Environment

○ Basic Pandas Concepts

2. **Data Structures in Pandas**

○ Understanding Series and DataFrames

○ Creating Series and DataFrames

○ Basic Operations with DataFrames

3. **Data Importing and Exporting**

○ Reading Data from Various Sources (CSV, Excel, SQL)

○ Exporting Data to Different Formats

4. **Data Cleaning and Preparation**

○ Handling Missing Data

○ Data Transformation

○ Filtering and Sorting Data

○ Data Type Conversions

5. **Data Analysis and Exploration**

○ Basic Statistics with Pandas

○ Grouping and Aggregating Data

○ Pivot Tables and Cross Tabulations

○ Time Series Analysis

6. **Advanced Data Manipulation**

○ Merging and Joining DataFrames

○ Reshaping and Pivoting

○ Advanced Filtering Techniques

○ Working with Text Data

7. **Data Visualization with Pandas**

○ Introduction to Data Visualization

○ Plotting with Pandas

○ Customizing Plots

8. **Real-World Projects and Case Studies**

○ Project 1: Analyzing Financial Data

○ Project 2: Data Analysis in Retail

○ Project 3: Time Series Forecasting

9. **Performance Tuning and Scaling Pandas**

○ Optimizing Pandas Code

○ Working with Large Datasets

○ Integration with Dask for Parallel Computing

10. **Best Practices and Tips**

○ Writing Efficient Pandas Code

○ Common Pitfalls and How to Avoid Them

○ Resources for Further Learning

11. **Appendix**

○ Glossary of Terms

○ References and Further Reading

12. **Index**

This index provides a structured layout to navigate through the course book, allowing quick access to specific topics or sections as needed.

About the Author

Have an extensive experience in analyzing, designing, implementing, and managing systems. Participated in a variety of commercial and industry projects, including healthcare consulting, construction industry solutions, financial institutions, banking, ticketing, interactive television, competitiveness analysis, business analysis, and others. Creator of the website https://cantinhode.net to help the coding community grow and to share insights about coding. The website includes opinion articles, practical examples, all with the goal of encouraging the development of technical solutions for information systems architecture across various domains, programming languages and on-premises and cloud solutions.

Read more at https://cantinhode.net.